Grammar: Grades 3–4

Table of Contents

Printed in the USA • All rights reserved.

ISBN 978-1-60418-260-6

Ready-to-Use Ideas and Activities

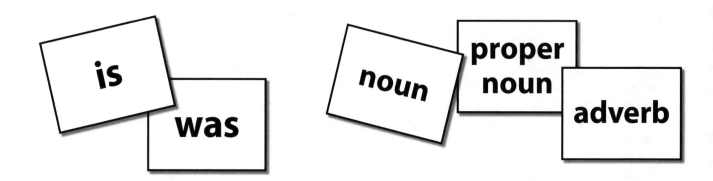

The activities in this book have been developed to help students master the basic skills necessary to succeed in grammar. These skills include learning about basic parts of speech, sentence components, and other word-study skills such as synonyms and antonyms. The activities have been sequenced to help ensure successful completion of the assigned tasks, thus building positive self-esteem, as well as the self-confidence students need to meet academic challenges. The activities may be used by themselves, as supplemental activities, or as enrichment material for a grammar program.

As you read through the activities listed below and go through this book, remember that all children learn at their own rate. Although repetition is important, it is critical that we keep sight of the fact that it is equally important to build children's self-esteem and self-confidence to become successful learners. If you are working with a child at home, set up a quiet, comfortable environment where you will work. Make it a special time to which you each look forward. Do only a few activities at a time and end each session on a positive note.

Flash Card Ideas

Cut apart the flash cards provided in the back of this book and use them for basic skill and enrichment activities. You can use them in the following ways or create your own way to use them.

- Write some or all of the flash card words on the board and divide students into groups. As students look at the list of words on the board, describe a word from the list. Begin with the part of speech, and then use synonyms, antonyms, spelling characteristics, a definition, how the word makes you feel, what kind of emotion it evokes, or anything else you can think of that describes the word. The team who correctly guesses the word first wins one point. After each word is guessed correctly, cross it off the list and go on to another. You can either have the group try to guess the word together or rotate guessers, giving everyone a chance. Continue playing to a certain number or only until one word remains.

Ready-to-Use Ideas and Activities

- Create a bingo sheet with five rows and five columns of blank squares. Write *FREE* in the middle square. Make enough copies to give one to each student. Write the flash card words as a list where students can see them. Have students choose 24 words from the list and write the words in the empty spaces of their bingo cards.

  When students have finished filling out their bingo cards, stack the flash cards into a deck. Call out the words one at a time. If a student has the word on his card, he should mark an *X* through the word to cross it out. The student who first crosses out five words in a row—horizontally, vertically, or diagonally—wins the game when she shouts, "Bingo!"

  To extend the game, continue playing until a student crosses out all of the words on his bingo sheet.

- Give each student three or four cards. Call out a part of speech (noun, verb, adjective, etc.) and have students hold up words that belong to that category.

- Have students categorize the words into designated groups. Use the categorized groups to create sentences.

- Have students alphabetize the cards as they read the words aloud.

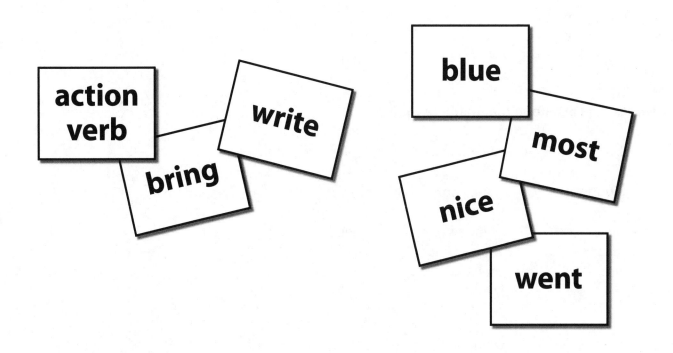

Common Nouns

A **common noun** is a word that names a person, place, or thing.
Examples: child (person), school (place), book (thing)

Underline each noun that names a person.

boy	friend	student
coach	secretary	game
both	jolly	teacher
house	sister	actor

Underline each noun that names a place.

science lab	classroom	food
playground	hallway	clinic
sun	paper	office
park	dog	diner

Underline each noun that names a thing.

desk	dictionary	ruler
neighbor	lunch box	city
house	window	book
truck	banana	teacher

CD-104310 • © Carson-Dellosa

Common Nouns

Complete each sentence by writing a noun that makes sense in each blank.

1. The _____ drove his _____ through the field.

2. The _____ went to the beach.

3. A nurse works in a _____.

4. The _____ blew in the wind.

5. My mom put a _____ in a jar.

6. The _____ belongs to _____.

7. A _____ tastes sweet.

8. The _____ broke down in the _____.

9. Taylor walked with his _____ to the _____.

10. Juan took a _____ to the park.

11. The _____ fell off the tree.

12. I always eat my snack in the _____.

Name _____

Proper Nouns

A **proper noun** is the name of a specific person, place, or thing. Begin all proper nouns with a capital letter.

Example: *Todd* took pictures of *Lookout Mountain* in *Tennessee*.

Underline the proper nouns in each sentence below.

1. The official address of the president of the United States is 1600 Pennsylvania Avenue.

2. The house at 1600 Pennsylvania Avenue used to be called the President's House.

3. The first president of the United States, George Washington, did not live in the President's House.

4. John Adams and his wife, Abigail, were the first to live there.

5. Soldiers from Great Britain burned the President's House during the War of 1812, so President Monroe lived near 20th Street for nine months.

6. Andrew Jackson had magnolia trees planted on the south lawn, called President's Park.

7. President Teddy Roosevelt changed the name of the house to the White House in 1901.

8. There was a second fire in the West Wing of the White House in 1929, while Herbert Hoover was president.

9. The inside of the White House was remodeled throughout much of President Harry S. Truman's term, so his family lived across Pennsylvania Avenue in the Blair House.

10. Another name for the White House is the Executive Mansion.

 CD-104310 • © Carson-Dellosa

Name _____

Proper Nouns

Circle the proper nouns in each sentence that need to begin with a capital letter.

1. My friends, jim and marty, want to join the boy scouts.

2. I heard ms. smith's class visited the lincoln memorial in washington, d.c.

3. Does your cousin mary go to winn school?

4. When his family was in idaho, mike floated down the snake river.

5. Last night, doug stopped at the brookstown mall to buy a gift.

6. Have you visited niagara falls in new york?

7. Yesterday, dana and her sister meg attended a party at the natural science museum.

8. When did avery and raul watch the baseball game at bryant stadium?

Write two sentences about specific places you have visited.

9. _____

_____

_____

10. _____

_____

_____

Singular and Plural Nouns

> A **singular noun** names one person, place, or thing.
>
>   Examples: violinist, stage, violin
>
> A **plural noun** names more than one person, place, or thing. Plural nouns often end in *s* or *es*.
>
>   Examples: violinists, stages, violins

Write *S* for each singular noun and *P* for each plural noun.

People

1. _____ child

2. _____ friends

3. _____ teammates

4. _____ neighbor

5. _____ workers

6. _____ guests

7. _____ mother

8. _____ partner

Places

9. _____ skyscraper

10. _____ factories

11. _____ hospital

12. _____ beaches

13. _____ gym

14. _____ restaurant

15. _____ hotels

16. _____ capitol

Things

17. _____ sailboats

18. _____ ramp

19. _____ parachute

20. _____ computers

Name _____

Plural Nouns

> If a noun ends with a vowel followed by *y*, add *s* to make it plural.
>
> Example: one day ⟶ two days
>
> If a noun ends with a consonant followed by *y*, change the *y* to *i* and add *es* to make it plural.
>
> Example: one baby ⟶ two babies

Write the plural form of each word.

1. bay

   _____

2. try

   _____

3. ray

   _____

4. candy

   _____

5. city

   _____

6. sky

   _____

7. monkey

   _____

8. day

   _____

9. lady

   _____

10. key

    _____

11. play

    _____

12. puppy

    _____

Name _____

Plural Nouns

> If a noun ends in *x, ch,* or *sh,* add *es* to make it plural.

Write either *s* or *es* to make each word plural.

1. fox

_____

2. book

_____

3. shoe

_____

4. stereo

_____

5. bicycle

_____

6. brush

_____

7. necklace

_____

8. vacation

_____

9. bunch

_____

10. box

_____

11. calendar

_____

12. photograph

_____

 CD-104310 • © Carson-Dellosa

Plural Nouns

> If a word ends in *f* or *fe,* change *f* or *fe* to *v* before adding *es.*
>
> Examples: *one* wolf ⟶ *two* wolves
>
> *one* life ⟶ *two* lives

Write the plural form of each word.

1. loaf   _____

2. half   _____

3. shelf   _____

4. calf   _____

5. knife   _____

6. leaf   _____

7. scarf   _____

8. hoof   _____

9. wife   _____

10. self   _____

11. life   _____

12. thief   _____

Name _____

Irregular Plural Nouns

Some nouns have irregular plural forms.
Examples: man → men
moose → moose

Draw a line to match each singular noun to its irregular plural form.

Singular	Plural	Singular	Plural
1. cactus	feet	5. child	mice
2. deer	deer	6. goose	women
3. foot	oxen	7. mouse	children
4. ox	cacti	8. woman	geese

Rewrite each sentence with the plural form of each underlined noun.

9. The <u>man</u> chased the <u>ox</u> down the road.

_____

_____

10. The <u>woman</u> and the <u>child</u> fed the <u>goose</u>.

_____

_____

Name _____

Possessive Nouns

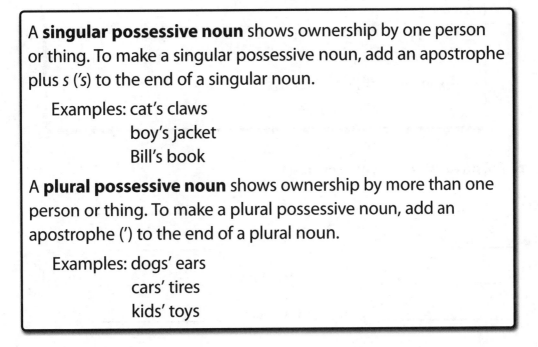

A **singular possessive noun** shows ownership by one person or thing. To make a singular possessive noun, add an apostrophe plus *s* ('s) to the end of a singular noun.

Examples: cat's claws
boy's jacket
Bill's book

A **plural possessive noun** shows ownership by more than one person or thing. To make a plural possessive noun, add an apostrophe (') to the end of a plural noun.

Examples: dogs' ears
cars' tires
kids' toys

Circle the possessive noun in each sentence. Then, circle *S* if the possessive noun is singular or *P* if the possessive noun is plural.

1. Mary's pet bird knows 12 words.   S   P

2. The girls' dresses were all very pretty.   S   P

3. Many of the stadium's seats needed painting.   S   P

4. Why were the books' pages ripped out?   S   P

Write apostrophes in the correct places in each sentence.

5. Did Jims dad talk to the teams coaches?

6. Some of the ladies golf clubs were bent or broken.

7. The skiers helmet was red and white.

8. Grants baseball glove was left in Matts car.

Possessive Nouns

For irregular nouns with plural forms that do not end in *s*, add apostrophe plus *s* ('*s*) to make the noun possessive.

Examples: children's mittens
mice's tails

Write the plural possessive form of each noun.

1. officer _____

2. people _____

3. men _____

4. berries _____

5. frames _____

6. moose _____

7. reptiles _____

8. courses _____

Write each phrase below using a possessive noun for each underlined noun.

Example: the room of the boys ⟶ the boys' room

9. the dance of the <u>ballerinas</u> _____

10. the taste of the <u>cookies</u> _____

11. the meeting of the <u>women</u> _____

12. the playground of the <u>children</u> _____

CD-104310 • © Carson-Dellosa

Possessive Nouns

Write the possessive form of each underlined word.

1. That is Danas dollhouse. _____

2. Craigs truck is big. _____

3. I like Sharons new green bicycle. _____

4. The childrens song was sung perfectly. _____

5. The two girls kites flew high in the sky. _____

6. The schools end-of-the-year picnic was fun. _____

7. The trains loud whistle scared Barbara. _____

8. The actors costume was colorful. _____

9. I love to visit my grandmothers house. _____

10. The singers voices are lovely. _____

11. The dogs collars are green. _____

12. Omar walked to his neighborhoods park. _____

Possessive Nouns

Example: Grandmothers glasses _____.
→ Grandmother's glasses fell off the chair.

Write an apostrophe in the correct place in each underlined word. Then, complete each sentence.

1. A <u>dolphins</u> fin _____.

2. <u>Janets</u> dimples _____.

3. The <u>roses</u> stems _____.

4. That <u>cars</u> wheels _____.

5. Two <u>robots</u> eyes _____.

6. <u>Kennys</u> bike _____.

7. <u>Lindas</u> doll _____.

8. <u>Marias</u> son _____.

9. Ten <u>girls</u> stickers _____.

10. Her three <u>kittens</u> toys _____.

Name _____

Pronouns

> A **pronoun** is a word that takes the place of a noun. *I, you, he, she, we, they, me, him, her, it, us,* and *them* are examples of pronouns.

Write the correct pronoun from the parentheses to complete each sentence.

1. Tia and _____ took the newspapers to the recycling center.
    (me, I)

2. Mark went to the store with _____.
    (me, I)

3. Bruce is going to Grandfather's farm next summer to visit _____.
    (he, him)

4. Do you have any coins you could give _____ for our collection?
    (us, we)

5. Lisa and Barry mowed the yard, so Dad gave _____ $3.00 each.
    (they, them)

6. Beto said _____ would meet us at the game.
    (he, him)

7. Maria realized she was late when _____ glanced at the clock.
    (she, her)

8. When _____ make hot chocolate, the water must be very hot.
    (us, we)

9. _____ took us to the basketball game after school.
    (They, Them)

10. Mom drove _____ dog to the veterinarian's office.
    (she, her)

Subject Pronouns

A **subject pronoun** is a word that can be used to replace the subject of a sentence. The subject of a sentence tells who or what the sentence is about. *You, I, he, she, it, we,* and *they* are examples of subject pronouns.

You and *I* can be used as the subject of a sentence.

Example: *You* and *I* enjoy watching bicycle races.

He, she, it, we, and *they* can replace nouns and phrases containing nouns in the subject part of a sentence.

Example: The Tour de France is a bicycle race. → *It* is a bicycle race.

Write the correct subject pronoun to replace each word or group of words.

1. scientists _____

2. Mr. Keller _____

3. mouth _____

4. the girl _____

5. our class _____

Rewrite each sentence. Replace each underlined word with the correct subject pronoun from the box.

they	he	she	it	we

6. Ms. Keller and her husband are marine biologists.

_____

7. My class heard them speak about squids.

_____

8. Giant squids live in the ocean.

_____

Object Pronouns

An **object pronoun** is a word that can replace a noun or a phrase in the predicate of a sentence. The predicate of a sentence is the part that includes the verb. An object pronoun receives the action of the verb. *Him, her, it, us,* and *them* are examples of object pronouns.

Example: Thunderstorms frighten my brother. → Thunderstorms frighten *him.*

Write the correct object pronoun to replace each word or group of words.

him	her	it	us	them

1. Carlos _____

2. Lisa _____

3. rain _____

4. lightning _____

5. clouds _____

6. water _____

7. Jack and me _____

8. sound waves _____

Rewrite each sentence. Replace each underlined word with the correct object pronoun from the box.

9. Mother called <u>Carlos and me</u> to come inside the house.

_____

10. Big, black clouds mean a <u>thunderstorm</u> is coming.

_____

11. We see flashes of lightning in <u>the clouds</u>.

_____

Object Pronouns

Read each pair of sentences. Complete the second sentence with the correct object pronoun.

1. Lisa received paint as a gift.

   Lisa received _____ as a gift.

2. She painted four pictures of Lucy and me.

   She painted four pictures of _____.

3. In one picture, she showed Lucy riding a bike.

   In one picture, she showed _____ riding a bike.

4. Then, she painted a picture of her dog and cat.

   Then, she painted a picture of _____.

5. Lisa hung her pictures up to dry.

   Lisa hung _____ up to dry.

6. She asked her mom and me to look at the pictures.

   She asked _____ to look at the pictures.

7. We liked the picture of the dog and cat best.

   We liked the picture of _____ best.

8. Lisa's mom hung the picture on the refrigerator.

   Lisa's mom hung _____ on the refrigerator.

CD-104310 • © Carson-Dellosa

Name _____

Subject and Object Pronouns

Write a sentence for each pronoun in the box.

| he | me | us | she | him | you | it | her |

1. _____

_____

2. _____

_____

3. _____

_____

4. _____

_____

5. _____

_____

6. _____

_____

7. _____

_____

8. _____

_____

Possessive Pronouns

A **possessive pronoun** tells who or what has something or owns something. *His, her, my, your, our, their,* and *its* are examples of possessive pronouns.

Example: Betsy Griscom's family lived in Philadelphia. → *Her* family lived in Philadelphia.

Read each pair of sentences. Complete the second sentence with the correct possessive pronoun.

1. Betsy Griscom is a person from history.

   _____ family is known for living in a simple and peaceful way.

2. Betsy's parents had 17 children.

   They taught _____ children to help with the chores.

3. In 1773, Betsy married John Ross.

   _____ job was to cover furniture with fabric, so Betsy sewed a lot to help him.

4. General George Washington designed a flag for the colonies.

   He gave _____ sketch to Betsy Griscom Ross to sew.

5. Betsy created the first American flag.

   The flag served as a symbol of freedom to _____ citizens.

6. Today, the American flag has 50 stars, one for each state.

   _____ colors are red, white, and blue.

CD-104310 • © Carson-Dellosa

Possessive Pronouns

Write the possessive form of each underlined word.

1. <u>Mary's</u> science report was about aardvarks.   _____

2. <u>Aardvarks'</u> appearance may look strange to us.   _____

3. <u>Aardvarks'</u> bodies are arched, and they have long noses.   _____

4. An <u>aardvark's</u> ears are large, and <u>an aardvark's</u> tail is long.   _____

5. <u>An aardvark's</u> diet consists mostly of insects.   _____

6. <u>An aardvark's</u> claws are powerful.   _____

7. A <u>baby aardvark's</u> mother looks after the baby for about a year.   _____

8. <u>Mary's</u> next science report will be on anteaters.   _____

Possessive Pronouns

These possessive pronouns come before nouns and show ownership: *my, his, her, its, our, your,* and *their.*

Example: John's car is red. → *His* car is red.

These possessive pronouns also can be used alone: *his, hers, its.*

Example: That is Anne's doll. → That is *hers.*

These possessive pronouns are always used alone: *mine, ours, yours,* and *theirs.*

Example: That is my basketball. → That is *mine.*

Read each pair of sentences. Complete the second sentence with the correct possessive pronoun.

1. Mrs. Atkins is the children's teacher.

   Mrs. Atkins is _____ teacher.

2. Mrs. Atkins's hair is red.

   _____ hair is red.

3. The desk next to the pencil sharpener is Mario's.

   It is _____.

4. Paul put his lunch box on the table.

   "This lunch box is _____," he said.

5. It is Ingrid and Juan's responsibility to keep the bookshelves neat.

   The responsibility is _____.

6. "We like this classroom," said the children.

   "It is _____ classroom," they said.

Name _____

Action Verbs

> An **action verb** tells what someone or something is doing.
> Examples: The boy *swings* the golf club.
> The mouse *scampers* across the floor.

Circle the action verb in each sentence.

1. Waldo hides from his friend.

2. James dashes behind the tree.

3. Marshall searches for the others.

4. Helen sits under the swing.

5. Jane kneels behind the slide.

6. Sam crawls along the fence.

7. Marshall finds Karen.

8. Karen races for the free spot.

9. Marshall tags Karen.

10. Karen calls for everyone to come out.

Action Verbs

Write an action verb that makes sense in each phrase.

1. _____ three fish

2. _____ for a clue

3. _____ a fun game

4. _____ the ball

5. _____ the milk

6. _____ the bike

7. _____ four cookies

8. _____ through the magnifying glass

9. _____ a question

10. _____ a log cabin

11. _____ the baseball game

12. _____ the flower seeds

13. _____ the picture

14. _____ in the pool

15. _____ a new coat

16. _____ the buttons

17. _____ the apple

18. _____ the red wagon

19. _____ a good story

20. _____ a pretty picture

Present Tense Action Verbs

A **present tense action verb** shows action that is happening now. When the noun in the subject of a sentence is singular, present tense action verbs often end in *s* or *es*.

Example: Stuart *reads* a book about a starfish.

Write the present tense action verb from the parentheses to complete each sentence.

1. A starfish _____ in the sea.
   (lived, lives)

2. It _____ one five-pointed star with its arms.
   (forms, formed)

3. Its arms _____ one foot across.
   (stretches, stretch)

4. If the starfish _____ an arm, it grows a new one!
   (injured, injures)

5. The starfish _____ along the bottom of the sea.
   (crawled, crawls)

6. It _____ on little tube feet on its underside.
   (moved, moves)

7. The starfish _____ for something to eat.
   (searches, searched)

8. It _____ some tasty fish.
   (spies, spied)

Name _____

Past Tense Action Verbs

A **past tense action verb** shows action that has already happened. The past tense of most action verbs is made by adding *ed* to the present tense verb.

Example: help ⟶ helped

Write the past tense of the underlined word in each sentence.

1. I <u>need</u> new shoes. _____

2. The shoes at the store <u>look</u> comfortable. _____

3. I <u>pick</u> the tennis shoes. _____

4. I <u>walk</u> in them. _____

5. My sister <u>wants</u> to borrow them. _____

6. She <u>attempts</u> to put them on her feet. _____

7. They <u>squash</u> her toes. _____

Complete each sentence. Use at least one past tense action verb in each sentence.

8. Last night, I _____.

9. This morning, I _____.

10. I _____ last week.

11. I _____ before I went to school.

12. Sam _____ us cookies at lunch.

Name _____

Past Tense Action Verbs

> Remember, most past tense action verbs are made by adding *ed* to the present tense verb.
>
> Example: help —► helped
>
> If the verb ends in a silent *e,* drop the *e* and add *ed.*
>
> Example: like —► liked
>
> If the verb ends with a single consonant after a single vowel, double the consonant and add *ed.*
>
> Example: plan —► planned
>
> If the verb ends in a consonant and *y,* change the *y* to *i* and add *ed.*
>
> Example: carry —► carried

Write the past tense form of each underlined action verb.

1. They <u>study</u> at the town library.   _____

2. The peacocks <u>show</u> their beautiful feathers.   _____

3. The children <u>like</u> the music.   _____

4. Beavers <u>flap</u> their tails on the water to signal danger.   _____

5. Some monkeys <u>curl</u> their tails around a branch.   _____

6. The people <u>hurry</u> inside before the rain started.   _____

7. Mel and Vanessa <u>stop</u> at the crosswalk.   _____

8. They <u>wait</u> for the school bus.   _____

Past Tense Action Verbs

Write the past tense form of each present tense verb.

Present Tense   **Past Tense**

1. glide   _____

2. invent   _____

3. dream   _____

4. cry   _____

5. spot   _____

6. guess   _____

7. hurry   _____

8. report   _____

Write two sentences with past tense action verbs.

9. _____

   _____

   _____

10. _____

   _____

   _____

Name _____

Past Tense Action Verbs

Write the past tense form of each underlined action verb.

1. A tadpole <u>hatches</u> from an egg in a pond.   _____

2. It <u>looks</u> like a small fish at first.   _____

3. The tadpole <u>uses</u> its tail to swim.   _____

4. It <u>breathes</u> with gills.   _____

5. Its appearance <u>changes</u> after a few weeks.   _____

6. It <u>starts</u> to grow hind legs.   _____

7. Its head <u>flattens</u>.   _____

8. Its gills <u>vanish</u>.   _____

Future Tense Verbs

A **future tense verb** shows action that has not happened yet. It tells about action that will or may happen in the future. The future tense often includes helping verbs like *will* and *might* in front of a main verb.

Examples: We *will go* to school tomorrow.
I *might take* ballet lessons.

Write *F* in front of each sentence with a future tense verb. Then, rewrite the sentences that are not marked with *F* in the future tense.

_____ 1. He is coming to my house to play.

_____ 2. They will bring cookies to the picnic.

_____ 3. I will be the line leader tomorrow.

_____ 4. Terry sings with the music.

_____ 5. Billy is listening to the radio.

_____ 6. Jill and Nan might go to the fair next week.

_____

_____

_____

_____

Future Tense Verbs

Write the future tense verb from the parentheses to complete each sentence.

1. Mary _____ dinner tonight.
   (will cook, cooked)

2. Angelo _____ his stepmom this weekend.
   (visit, might visit)

3. Carrie _____ to the movies tomorrow.
   (might go, went)

4. Scott _____ his new book this evening.
   (is reading, will read)

5. Wendy _____ me her new bracelet when she returns.
   (showed, will show)

6. You and I _____ in the park tomorrow.
   (could play, played)

Read each pair of sentences. Circle the sentence that shows future tense.

7. Bob ran to the market.   Bob will run around the block.

8. I am having green beans with dinner.   I will have corn tomorrow.

9. Troy will catch the ball.   Troy catches the ball.

10. He may go to the new school.   He went to the new school.

11. Davion washed the dog.   Davion will wash the dog.

12. She will walk home.   She walks home.

Past, Present, and Future Tense Verbs

Remember, verb tenses tell when something is happening.

Underline the verb in each sentence. If the verb is future tense, underline both the main verb and the helping verb before it. Circle *past*, *present*, **or** *future* **to show the tense of the verb.**

1. Vanessa signed her name on the card.	past	present	future
2. Greg will golf in the tournament.	past	present	future
3. Megan snaps the links together.	past	present	future
4. Brant climbs into his bed.	past	present	future
5. Layne will set her alarm clock.	past	present	future
6. Kallie rocked her puppy to sleep.	past	present	future
7. Jill will dip the strawberries in chocolate.	past	present	future
8. Raymond catches a fish.	past	present	future
9. Jade calculated the answer.	past	present	future
10. Fran will ace the test.	past	present	future
11. Ava writes her article.	past	present	future
12. Mel dined with her guests.	past	present	future

Irregular Verbs

Remember, most past tense verbs are formed by adding *ed* to the present tense form of the verb. The past tense of irregular verbs is not formed in this way.

Example: I *see* the red car. (present tense)

I *saw* the red car yesterday. (past tense)

Write the past tense of each irregular verb. Look up the present tense verb in a dictionary to learn the past tense, if needed.

Present Tense	Past Tense	Present Tense	Past Tense
1. write	_____	6. teach	_____
2. draw	_____	7. find	_____
3. speak	_____	8. feel	_____
4. hold	_____	9. bend	_____
5. hear	_____	10. catch	_____

Write the past tense form of each underlined word.

11. I <u>see</u> a butterfly on a flower.   _____

12. The butterfly <u>makes</u> her egg sticky.   _____

13. The tiny white egg <u>sticks</u> to the leaf.   _____

14. A small caterpillar <u>comes</u> out of the egg.   _____

Helping Verbs with Main Verbs

A **helping verb** is a verb that helps the main verb express or show a tense.

There are 23 helping verbs:

> be, being, been
> am, is, are, was, were
> do, does, did
> have, has, had
> may, must, might
> can, could
> will, would
> shall, should

Up to three helping verbs can be used at one time.

Examples: Annette *was* crying.
Pete *should have* cut the grass.
Dottie *will have been* sleeping for an hour.

Circle the helping verb or verbs in each sentence. Then, draw an arrow to the main verb.

1. The animal is being protected by the cactus.

2. The tiles are being hung behind the sink.

3. Those fossils may have been left by a dinosaur.

4. Toothbrushes should be replaced after you are sick.

5. Becky and Irene will be using the gym in that building.

6. The squirrel could have been hurt if it fell.

7. Nick and Luke were picking strawberries.

8. We may be going to the beach.

Helping Verbs with Irregular Verbs

Many past tense verbs used with the helping verbs *has* and *have* are formed by adding *ed* to the present tense form of the verb. Irregular verbs do not follow this rule.

Examples: I *see* him. (present)
I *saw* him. (past)
I *have seen* him before. (past with a helping verb)

Write the missing form of each irregular verb. Refer to a dictionary, if necessary.

Present	Past	Past with Has or Have
1. sing	_____	has or have sung
2. tell	told	has or have _____
3. _____	brought	has or have brought
4. wear	wore	has or have _____
5. take	_____	has or have taken
6. _____	stood	has or have stood

Write the past tense form of each irregular verb in parentheses.

7. Our teacher has _____ our class a book about insects.
(read)

8. I had _____ Mr. Lee before he was my teacher.
(know)

9. Ms. Kemp had _____ us that we could eat outside today.
(tell)

10. Drew has _____ that I can borrow his jump rope anytime.
(say)

11. I had _____ that sunglasses protect your eyes.
(hear)

12. Scientists have _____ that insects cannot move or focus their eyes.
(show)

Linking Verbs

A **linking verb** is a verb that does not show action. A linking verb connects, or links, two parts of a sentence. Many linking verbs are forms of the verb *be*.

There are eight forms of the verb *be*:

am, are, is, was, were, (will) be, (am, are, was, were) being, (have, has, had) been

Examples: I *am* left-handed.
He *is* an artist.
You *are* a gymnast.
We *will be* best friends.

Circle the linking verb in each sentence.

1. I am a scientist who studies insects.

2. Insects are the most plentiful creatures on Earth.

3. I have a lot of information to share about insects.

4. A honeycomb cell is a home for one honeybee egg.

5. Monarchs are migrating butterflies.

6. A bee is a flying insect that can sting you.

7. A moth is different from a butterfly.

8. All ladybugs are not female.

9. Spiders are not insects.

10. A pupa is a stage in an insect's life.

11. Who knew there was so much to learn about insects?

CD-104310 • © Carson-Dellosa

Linking Verbs

Seem, appear, and become are also linking verbs.

Circle the linking verb in each sentence.

1. Mary was happy when her friends attended her dance performance.

2. Kelsey seems sorry she missed the party.

3. Mysteries are my favorite type of book.

4. Today is the third Monday of January.

5. The team appears pleased with the game.

6. Kay was amused when Ken told jokes.

7. I become anxious when I don't finish my homework before dinner.

8. Mr. Alton was quiet during the concert.

9. The students were happy with their grades.

10. She had a fabulous time at the party.

11. I am walking home after school.

12. Dominic will practice the piano today.

Present Tense Action Verbs and Linking Verbs

Remember, a present tense action verb shows action that is happening now. Present tense action verbs end in *s* or *es* when the noun in the subject is singular.

Example: It jumps.

Also remember, a linking verb does not show action. It links two parts of a sentence.

Example: It *is* funny.

Write *A* for each present tense action verb and *L* for each linking verb.

1. bloom _____   11. appears _____

2. scream _____   12. hatch _____

3. seems _____   13. is _____

4. has _____   14. stir _____

5. have _____   15. study _____

6. pretend _____   16. hold _____

7. becomes _____   17. am _____

8. walk _____   18. was _____

9. were _____   19. jump _____

10. skip _____   20. scatter _____

Present Tense Action Verbs and Linking Verbs

Write the correct present tense action or linking verb from the parentheses to complete each sentence.

1. The jumping bean _____ a seed of a Mexican bush.
   (is, are)

2. A person actually can _____ the seed jump.
   (see, sees)

3. First, a moth _____ its eggs on the bush's flowers.
   (lay, lays)

4. The eggs _____ , and caterpillars emerge.
   (hatch, hatches)

5. The caterpillars _____ into the bush's seeds.
   (burrow, burrows)

6. The caterpillar _____ the inside of the seed, leaving the outer shell.
   (eat, eats)

7. Then, it _____ a web inside the hollow seed.
   (build, builds)

8. The caterpillar _____ the web and wiggles its body.
   (grab, grabs)

9. The seed _____ !
   (jump, jumps)

10. The jumping bean _____ active for several months.
    (appear, appears)

Past Tense Action Verbs and Linking Verbs

Remember, a past tense action verb shows action that has already happened.

Example: I *learned* about George Washington Carver yesterday.

The past tense forms of the linking verb *be* are *was* and *were*.

Example: I *was* at the party.

The past tense form of the linking verb *have* is *had*.

Example: I *had* three beans left on my plate.

The past tense form of the linking verb *become* is *became*.

Example: His research *became* important.

Write *A* for each sentence with a past tense action verb and *L* for each sentence with a past tense linking verb.

1. _____ George Washington Carver was an American scientist.

2. _____ He became famous for his agricultural research.

3. _____ Carver discovered more than 300 products from peanuts.

4. _____ He had more than 75 products from pecans.

5. _____ He developed more than 100 products from sweet potatoes.

6. _____ Carver encouraged southern farmers to try growing new crops.

7. _____ He taught farmers about keeping their crops healthy.

8. _____ Carver was head of a large research group.

9. _____ He received many awards for his contributions to science.

CD-104310 • © Carson-Dellosa

Name _____

Forms of *Be*

> The verb *be* is special because it has many forms.
>
> When the subject of the sentence is singular, the verb *be* uses the form *am, is,* or *was.*
>
> > Examples: John *is* my brother.
> >
> > I *am* nine years old.
> >
> > Mrs. Taylor *was* my teacher.
>
> When the subject is plural, or if the subject is you, the verb *be* uses the form *are* or *were.*
>
> > Examples: We *are* best friends.
> >
> > Dan and Amy *were* on the bus.
> >
> > You *are* a good student.
>
> Remember, sometimes the forms of *be* are used as helping verbs.
>
> > Examples: We *were eating* dinner.
> >
> > I *am walking* the dog.

Write the correct present tense form of the verb *be* to complete each sentence.

1. Mandy _____ my next-door neighbor.

2. The Taylors _____ on vacation.

3. You _____ a great friend.

4. I _____ the oldest in my family.

Write the correct past tense form of the verb *be* to complete the sentences.

5. Bill and Sue _____ at the movies.

6. Mom _____ at work yesterday.

7. I _____ at my aunt's house.

8. You _____ very helpful today.

Forms of *Be*

Be, being, and *been* are forms of the verb *be* used only after a helping verb.

> Examples: Dad *will be* here in a minute.
> They *were being* very polite.
> I *have been* to the doctor.

Sometimes, these forms of *be* are used as helping verbs before the main verb in a sentence.

> Examples: We *will be camping* at the lake.
> She *was being taken* to the office.
> Jeff *has been writing* a story.

Write the correct form of the verb *be* from the parentheses to complete the sentence.

1. The Gibsons have _____ to the fair.
   (been, being)

2. Rick is _____ nice to me.
   (being, be)

3. You must _____ hungry.
   (be, been)

4. The girls might _____ walking home.
   (be, being)

Write four sentences that each use the subject *I* but use different forms of the verb *be*.

5. _____

6. _____

7. _____

8. _____

Adjectives

An **adjective** is a word that describes a noun. An adjective tells how many or what kind. An adjective often comes in front of the noun it describes.

> Examples: *Two* prairie dogs live in a burrow. (*Two* tells how many.)
> *Little* prairie dogs are called pups. (*Little* tells what kind.)

An adjective can come after a linking verb.

> Example: The prairie dog is *little*. (*Little* tells what kind.)

A sentence may have more than one adjective.

> Examples: The *two* prairie dogs are *little*.
> The *two little* prairie dogs are called pups.

Circle the adjective that describes each underlined noun.

1. The prairie dog lives in a small <u>burrow</u> under the ground.

2. She makes a nest of dried <u>plants</u> in the spring.

3. The prairie dog gives birth to a litter of four <u>pups</u>.

4. She is a good <u>mother</u> and stays close to her babies.

5. The pups are ready to venture outside after six <u>weeks</u>.

6. The pups have many <u>friends</u>.

Adjectives

Underline the adjectives in each paragraph.

1. I like chocolate ice cream. Chocolate ice cream is good when it is hot outside. Unfortunately, chocolate ice cream makes a big, sticky mess. I solved this problem by eating my yummy chocolate ice cream outside.

2. One sunny day, I saw my neighbor's white rabbit hopping in front of my house. The rabbit seemed scared. I walked up to my neighbor's rabbit and talked to him. He hopped over to me, and I picked him up. His soft fur tickled my hands. I took the sweet rabbit home to my neighbor's house. My neighbor was happy to see his rabbit safe. The rabbit was happy to be home too.

3. Anna went to a big shoe store with her mother. Anna needed some new shoes. She saw black, shiny shoes and white shoes with ruffles. Anna especially liked the fancy red dress shoes with black and white trim. Anna decided to buy some tan shoes. Anna's mother paid the tall salesman, and Anna wore her new shoes home.

4. Shawn drove his rusty old truck home through the rain. Its tired engine rumbled, and the loud sound echoed throughout the small, quiet neighborhood. As he pulled into his wet driveway, he listened to the large drops of rain bounce on the aging metal.

Name _____

Adjectives That Compare

An adjective can be used to compare nouns. Add *er* to adjectives to compare two nouns. Add *est* to compare more than two nouns.

    Examples: bright → brighter → brightest

If an adjective ends with *e,* drop the *e* and add *er* to compare two nouns. Drop the *e* and add *est* to compare more than two nouns.

    Examples: white → whiter → whitest

If an adjective ends in a consonant that comes after a short vowel, double the final consonant and add *er* or *est*.

    Examples: thin → thinner → thinnest

Write the correct forms of each adjective.

Adjectives	Adjectives That Compare Two Nouns	Adjectives That Compare More Than Two Nouns
1. long	_____	_____
2. soft	_____	_____
3. large	_____	_____
4. flat	_____	_____
5. sweet	_____	_____
6. wide	_____	_____
7. cool	_____	_____
8. smart	_____	_____

Proper Adjectives

A **proper adjective** is a word made from a proper noun. Proper adjectives begin with capital letters and describe nouns.

> Example: The *New York* skyline is beautiful at night. (*New York* is a proper noun, but here it is used as an adjective to describe the skyline.)

Some proper adjectives are made by adding an ending to a proper noun.

> Example: We ate at a *Chinese* restaurant in New York City. (*Chinese* is made from the proper noun *China*).

Write *PA* if the underlined word or words are used as proper adjectives. Write *PN* if they are used as proper nouns.

_____ 1. There are many <u>Puerto Rican</u> neighborhoods in New York City.

_____ 2. Some people have recently arrived from <u>Puerto Rico</u>.

_____ 3. Years ago, many <u>Irish</u> immigrants moved to America.

_____ 4. They came from <u>Ireland</u> in the 1800s and 1900s.

_____ 5. <u>German</u> people immigrated to America, also.

_____ 6. Some of the first <u>English</u> settlers were the Puritans.

_____ 7. They left <u>England</u> for several reasons in the 1600s.

_____ 8. Many people from <u>Asian</u> cultures came to live on the West Coast.

_____ 9. There are many <u>Korean</u> communities in Southern California.

_____ 10. <u>American</u> culture has been formed from many different cultures.

Articles

> The words *a, an,* and *the* make up a special group of adjectives called articles. An **article** can be used before a noun or an adjective/noun combination in a sentence.
>
> Use *a* before a singular noun that begins with a consonant.
>
> Example: I saw *a* firefly.
>
> Use *an* before a singular noun that begins with a vowel.
>
> Example: Max brought *an* orange for lunch.
>
> Use *the* before singular or plural nouns that begin with any letter.
>
> Example: Ten apples are in *the* basket.

Circle the articles in each sentence. Underline the noun that follows each article.

1. Our dog sleeps in a doghouse.

2. The movie made us laugh.

3. I carried an umbrella in the rain.

4. Our boat had a leak.

5. Earth rotates around the sun.

6. I ate an apple and a sandwich for lunch.

7. Dad keeps the nails in an egg carton.

8. The books filled the shelf.

9. Rick saw a blue whale in the ocean.

10. An elephant likes to eat peanuts.

Articles

Complete each sentence with the correct article.

1. I enjoyed watching _____ game.

2. Would you like _____ egg sandwich?

3. I have _____ dog and _____ cat.

4. Did you hear _____ thunder?

5. An eagle flew over _____ house.

6. My grandmother gave me _____ new bike for my birthday.

7. The wind blew my umbrella down _____ street.

8. Mrs. Hayes said that I did _____ good job on my art project.

9. Was there _____ egg in her nest?

Write a sentence using each article.

10. a: _____

_____

11. an: _____

_____

12. the: _____

_____

Adverbs

> An **adverb** is a word that describes a verb. Adverbs tell how, when, where, or to what extent (how much or how long) something happens.
>
> Examples: The 100-meter dash starts tomorrow. (When?)
> That runner fell down. (Where?)
> The people taking tickets worked quickly. (How?)
> Marathon runners run far. (How long?)

Circle the adverb in each sentence. Underline the verb that the adverb describes.

1. Janice closes the book quickly.

2. Tito frequently plays in the park.

3. Missie will watch a movie tonight.

4. Zack worked quietly on his model.

5. Leo ran on the path yesterday.

6. Pete and Susie flew to their grandma's city today.

7. Walter will miss his game tomorrow.

8. Tracy mixed the ingredients carefully.

9. Rick will eat strawberries later.

10. Ariel often stops to pick flowers.

Adverbs

Circle the adverb in each sentence. Underline the verb that the adverb describes.

1. On Independence Day, we usually go to the parade.

2. We drive slowly because of the traffic.

3. The parade often begins with a marching band.

4. The marching band plays loudly.

5. The huge crowd cheers excitedly.

6. My favorite part is when the big floats pass near us.

7. All of the floats are decorated beautifully.

8. We never see one we do not like.

Write your own sentences using the given adverbs.

9. slowly: _____

_____

10. yesterday: _____

_____

11. away: _____

_____

12. there: _____

_____

Adverbs

Circle the adverb in each sentence. Underline the verb that the adverb describes.

1. The dogs bark loudly at the mail carrier.

2. I looked everywhere for my coat.

3. Nancy swims faster than I do.

4. Greg walked slowly.

5. Valerie awoke early.

6. Let's play inside.

Complete each sentence with the best *how* adverb from the box. Circle the verb that the adverb describes.

> quickly   beautifully   happily   better

7. The class worked _____ to finish the work before the bell.

8. I _____ ate my cookie.

9. I think carrots taste _____ than celery.

10. We sang _____.

Complete each sentence with the best *where* adverb from the box. Circle the verb that the adverb describes.

> above   inside   there   up

11. Carlos placed the book _____.

12. Donny is waiting _____ for his mom.

13. The plane is flying _____ the clouds.

14. Ping threw the ball _____ in the air.

Adverbs

Complete each sentence with the best *when* adverb from the box. Circle the verb that the adverb describes.

sometimes	now	yesterday

1. Sara left her shoes at the gym _____.

2. I like to go camping _____.

3. Since you are finished, can you help me _____?

Write one sentence using a *how* adverb, one sentence using a *where* adverb, and one sentence using a *when* adverb.

4. _____

5. _____

6. _____

Think of three different adverbs to complete this sentence:

Mark finished his homework _____.

Write your three new sentences below.

7. _____

8. _____

9. _____

Name _____

Adverbs That Compare

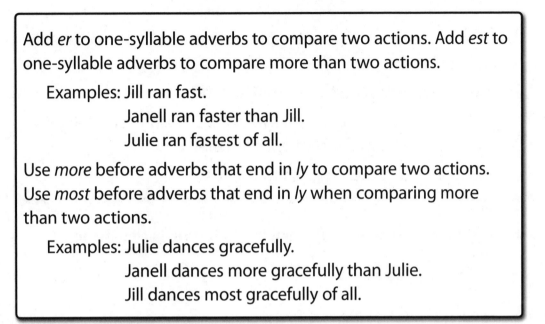

Add *er* to one-syllable adverbs to compare two actions. Add *est* to one-syllable adverbs to compare more than two actions.

    Examples: Jill ran fast.
              Janell ran faster than Jill.
              Julie ran fastest of all.

Use *more* before adverbs that end in *ly* to compare two actions. Use *most* before adverbs that end in *ly* when comparing more than two actions.

    Examples: Julie dances gracefully.
              Janell dances more gracefully than Julie.
              Jill dances most gracefully of all.

Write the correct forms of each adverb.

Adverbs	Adverbs That Compare Two Actions	Adverbs That Compare More Than Two Actions
1. quietly	_____	_____
2. strong	_____	_____
3. frequently	_____	_____
4. short	_____	_____

Complete each sentence with the correct adverb from the parentheses.

5. Mom, Tanya, and I waited _____ for Dad to arrive.
              (patiently, more patiently)

6. We clapped _____ for the other team.
      (enthusiastically, most enthusiastically)

7. You must drive _____ when the road is wet than when it is dry.
      (carefully, more carefully)

Simple Subjects and Predicates

The **simple subject** is a noun or pronoun that tells who or what a statement is about.

Example: Many *people* enjoy winter sports.

The **simple predicate** is an action verb or a linking verb that tells what the subject of the statement does or is.

Example: Skiers *glide* over snow on skis.

Circle the simple subject and underline the simple predicate in each sentence.

1. A snowmobile is a sled with a motor.

2. One or two people can ride on a snowmobile.

3. The driver steers with handlebars.

4. Some scientists believe that riding a snowmobile harms nature and animals.

5. A toboggan is another kind of sled.

6. Toboggans are long wooden sleds without a motor.

7. Usually four people ride a toboggan in a contest.

8. A driver steers the toboggan from the rear.

9. Snowboards look similar to skateboards without wheels.

10. Snowboarding became an Olympic event in 1998.

Name _____

Simple Subjects

Underline the simple subject in each sentence.

1. Astronauts are very brave people.

2. Donna's birthday is today.

3. The big, red boat raced across the water.

4. The spectators enjoyed the fireworks.

5. Diego loves to garden.

6. The blue engine stopped at the station.

7. The actor was excellent in the play.

8. That movie was the best I have ever seen!

9. Good health is important.

10. The pictures in that book are beautiful.

11. Marta rides her bike.

12. The juicy apple tastes sweet.

Simple Predicates

Circle the simple predicate in each sentence.

1. Bess danced in the talent show.

2. We went to the mall after the library.

3. California is a state on the West Coast.

4. The weather began to turn cool.

5. It rained for hours yesterday!

6. Opal painted a picture for her mom.

7. Snow fell onto the frozen ground.

8. Seven students were in the spelling bee.

9. The tractor made a loud noise.

10. We served ice cream and cake at the party.

11. Mom made her famous fruit salad.

12. Daniel was a great listener.

CD-104310 • © Carson-Dellosa

Name _____

Complete Subjects and Predicates

> The **complete subject** of a sentence contains the simple subject and any words that complement it.
>
> Example: *The animal with the largest ears* is the African elephant.
>
> The **complete predicate** of a sentence contains the simple predicate and any words that complement it.
>
> Example: Ruffles *is the name of my dog.*

Draw a line under the complete subject in each sentence. Circle each complete predicate.

1. That mug is from my family's trip last summer.

2. Ben's stepdad drove to the grocery store.

3. Ms. Nelson hung a swing on her porch.

4. This kind of plastic can be recycled.

5. White peaches are sold at the store now.

6. Carmen heard the new song on the radio.

7. My teacher explained several scientific ideas.

8. Tina's friend, Heather, made dumplings for dinner.

9. This fly will not stop bothering me!

10. The back door is unlocked.

Complete Subjects

Underline the complete subject in each sentence. Circle each simple subject.

1. A giant tortoise may live 100 years.

2. Baby pandas are completely white at birth.

3. Some mammals spend 12 hours a day eating.

4. An alligator's eye has three eyelids.

5. Giraffes have the same number of neck bones as humans.

6. A sloth may spend its whole life in one tree.

7. An elephant's trunk has 40,000 muscles.

8. An octopus is a shy sea creature.

9. Octopuses grow new tentacles if they lose any.

10. A chameleon's tongue is as long as its body.

11. Dolphin brains weigh more than human brains.

12. A hummingbird can fly straight up.

Complete Predicates

Underline the complete predicate in each sentence. Circle each simple predicate.

1. The squirrel lives in my backyard.

2. He awakens in his leafy nest early in the morning.

3. The rest of his family left earlier to look for food.

4. The squirrel races along the elm's branches.

5. The squirrel scampers down the tree trunk.

6. He searches for some seeds he had buried.

7. His good sense of smell helps him find them.

8. The squirrel spies his brothers nearby.

9. They chatter back and forth.

10. Then, they chase one another all around.

11. Soon, the squirrel tires of the game.

12. He stretches out in the warm sun to rest.

Compound Subjects and Predicates

A **compound subject** has two or more simple subjects joined by *and*.

> Example: The *climate* and *plants* on Earth changed at the end of the Ice Age.
> (The sentence has two simple subjects.)

A **compound predicate** has two or more simple predicates joined by *and*.

> Example: Trees *grew* and *covered* the land with thick forests.
> (The sentence has two simple predicates.)

Write *CS* if the sentence has a compound subject. Write *CP* if it has a compound predicate. Write *N* if the sentence has neither a compound subject nor a compound predicate.

1. _____ Stone Age farmers cut and cleared trees from the forests.

2. _____ They used stone axes and picks.

3. _____ Wood and deer antlers were used for handles on tools.

4. _____ Tree trunks and large branches were used to build shelters.

5. _____ People also made canoes from the tree trunks.

6. _____ People and animals needed water to survive.

7. _____ Communities were often started near rivers and lakes.

8. _____ People caught fish and traveled on the water.

9. _____ Stone Age people used fire for cooking.

10. _____ They rubbed two pieces of flint together and made a spark to start a fire.

11. _____ Farmers harvested their crops and kept seeds for planting next year.

12. _____ Hunting and fishing were important to farmers.

Subject/Verb Agreement

The verb in the predicate of a sentence must agree with the subject of the sentence.

If the subject is singular, add *s* to most present tense verbs.

Example: Pollution *harms* animals and plants.

If the subject is plural, the main present tense verb does not change.

Example: People *cause* most of the pollution.

Write the verb in parentheses that agrees with the subject of each sentence.

1. Oceans _____ more than seven-tenths of Earth's surface.
    (covers, cover)

2. Oceans _____ over 90 percent of Earth's water.
    (contain, contains)

3. More than half of the people on Earth _____ near the ocean.
    (live, lives)

4. An enormous amount of food _____ from the oceans.
    (come, comes)

5. Pollution _____ the animals that live in the sea.
    (hurt, hurts)

6. Chemicals used in farming _____ the rivers.
    (pollute, pollutes)

7. Rivers _____ these chemicals to the oceans.
    (carry, carries)

8. People _____ trash and litter into the oceans.
    (toss, tosses)

9. Trash _____ problems for sea animals.
    (create, creates)

10. The government _____ throwing trash in the oceans.
    (forbid, forbids)

Subject/Verb Agreement

A compound subject is like a plural subject. It has two or more simple subjects joined by *and*. The main present tense verb does not change.

Example: The saguaro and other cactuses *produce* flowers.

Add *s* to most present tense verbs when the subject pronoun is *she, he,* or *it*.

Example: She *grows* cactuses.

The main verb does not change when the subject pronoun is *I, we, you,* or *they*.

Example: They *grow* flowers.

Write the verb that agrees with the subject of each sentence.

1. Most cacti _____ in hot, dry places.
   (grow, grows)

2. They _____ in size and shape.
   (vary, varies)

3. The height of some cacti _____ 60 feet.
   (reach, reaches)

4. Some varieties of cacti _____ like porcupines.
   (look, looks)

5. Thick, fleshy stems and long roots _____ cacti survive.
   (help, helps)

6. The stem _____ water.
   (hold, holds)

7. The cactus's waxy skin _____ water near the cactus.
   (keep, keeps)

8. Its long roots _____ water after a rain.
   (gather, gathers)

Name _____

Declarative and Interrogative Sentences

A **declarative sentence** tells something and ends with a period. It makes a statement.

Example: Animals live in each country.

An **interrogative sentence** asks a question and ends with a question mark.

Example: What kind of animals live in your country?

Add the correct punctuation mark at the end of each sentence. Answer the question with a declarative sentence using the information given.

1. Where do kangaroos live____

   Kangaroos live where koalas live____

   Koalas live in Australia____

   _____

2. Most wild penguins live south of the equator____

   Do wild penguins live in Antarctica____

   Antarctica is south of the equator____

   _____

3. Monarch butterflies migrate to Michigan in the spring____

   These butterflies migrate to Mexico in the fall____

   Are monarch butterflies in Michigan in the winter____

   _____

4. Do orangutans live in the Brazilian rain forest____

   The Brazilian rain forest is in South America____

   Orangutans live in a small part of Southeast Asia____

   _____

Exclamatory Sentences

> An **exclamatory sentence** shows strong feeling and ends with an exclamation mark.
>
>   Example: This is the best birthday ever!

Rewrite each exclamatory sentence. Add capital letters where they belong and exclamation marks at the end of each exclamatory sentence.

1. this dessert is delicious

   _____

2. that comet is beautiful

   _____

3. we're going to florida

   _____

4. ouch, get off my foot

   _____

5. you startled me

   _____

6. the fireworks are incredible

   _____

7. listen to that thunder

   _____

8. wow, your picture looks great

   _____

Name _____

Declarative, Interrogative, and Exclamatory Sentences

For each sentence, write *D* for declarative, *I* for interrogative, or *E* for exclamatory. Add the correct punctuation mark at the end of each sentence. Circle the letters that should be capitalized.

1. _____ our class is going to the amusement park___

2. _____ the bus will leave early___

3. _____ did you set your alarm clock___

4. _____ abby and I stood in line together___

5. _____ yikes, the food here is expensive___

6. _____ did you bring lunch___

7. _____ i'm glad I did___

8. _____ we put our lunches on the tables___

9. _____ let's go to the rides___

10. _____ mona, julie, max, and I got in line for a roller coaster___

11. _____ we put on our seat belts and harnesses___

12. _____ i'm scared___

Word Order in Sentences

Words in a sentence must be in the correct order to make sense.

Examples: Eight planets has known the solar system. (This sentence does not make sense.)

The solar system has eight known planets. (Changing the order of the same words makes the sentence make sense.)

The order of words in a sentence can determine whether a sentence is a declarative sentence or an interrogative sentence.

Examples: The solar system does have eight known planets. (The order of the words makes this a declarative sentence.)

Does the solar system have eight known planets? (The order of these same words makes this an interrogative sentence.)

Write each group of words in the correct order to form a declarative sentence.

1. Six moons that orbit them have planets. _____

_____

2. Their own light do not have planets. _____

3. Many rings it has around Saturn. _____

Reorder the words in each declarative sentence to write an interrogative sentence.

4. Saturn is the second largest planet. _____

5. You can see Saturn's rings with a telescope. _____

_____

6. Scientists are still studying Saturn. _____

Imperative Sentences

An **imperative sentence** is a sentence that gives a command. Most imperative sentences end with periods. Sometimes, a command is given with great feeling. In this case, an exclamation mark is used. The same command can end with either a period or an exclamation mark, depending on the situation.

Examples: Sit down. (Your mom is asking you to sit down to dinner.)

Sit down! (A person is standing on a chair.)

Read each sentence. Put the correct punctuation at the end of each imperative sentence.

1. Do not touch that____ The oven was just turned off and is extremely hot.

2. Do not touch that____ Dad put a bowl of carrots on the table for dinner.

3. Hold still____ A bee is flying near by.

4. Hold still____ Kyle is tying his brother's shoe.

5. Come here____ Lee's dog is wandering off.

6. Come here____ Maria wants to tell Steve something.

7. Shut the door____ Nan left the door open.

8. Shut the door____ Grant is having a surprise party for June.

9. Stop that____ A basketball is rolling slowly off the court.

10. Stop that____ Alex's full grocery cart is rolling away.

Name _____

The Four Types of Sentences

Remember, there are four kinds of sentences: declarative, interrogative, exclamatory, and imperative.

A declarative sentence tells something. It ends with a period.

An interrogative sentence asks something. It ends with a question mark.

An exclamatory sentence shows great emotion. It ends with an exclamation mark.

An imperative sentence gives an order. It ends with a period or an exclamation mark.

For each sentence, write *D* for declarative, *IN* for interrogative, *E* for exclamatory, or *IM* for imperative.

_____ 1. Whales must eat a lot.

_____ 2. Why do you think that?

_____ 3. Whales are the largest animals alive.

_____ 4. Blue whales can weigh up to 200 tons.

_____ 5. They are gigantic!

_____ 6. That is unbelievable!

_____ 7. Find out how much other animals eat.

_____ 8. How much does a lion eat?

_____ 9. They eat 50 or 60 pounds of meat daily.

_____ 10. A lion can eat that much at one meal!

Name _____

The Four Types of Sentences

For each sentence, write *D* for declarative, *IN* for interrogative, *E* for exclamatory, or *IM* for imperative. Add the correct punctuation mark at the end of each sentence.

1. _____ Carol lives in a pretty house____

2. _____ Does Kristy like peanut butter____

3. _____ I called Terry____

4. _____ Take Erik's cat to his house____

5. _____ Wow, Ryan hit a home run____

6. _____ Ouch, that hurt____

Write an example of each type of sentence.

7. Imperative: _____

_____

8. Exclamatory: _____

_____

9. Interrogative: _____

_____

10. Declarative: _____

_____

Name _____

Commas

Commas can be used to separate words in a series or list.

Example: Grapefruit, oranges, tangerines, and lemons are citrus fruits.

Rewrite each sentence below, using commas where they are needed.

1. My favorite sports are soccer basketball and tennis.

   _____

   _____

2. Remember to grab your lunch box book bag and raincoat for school.

   _____

   _____

3. I want cheese garlic and green pepper on my pizza.

   _____

   _____

4. My duties are to dust feed the cat and take out the trash.

   _____

   _____

5. Please stop by the store for cereal milk and orange juice.

   _____

   _____

 CD-104310 • © Carson-Dellosa

Commas

A comma or commas can be used to set apart the name of the person being spoken to directly from the rest of the sentence.

> Examples: Where can I learn more about falcons, Alex?
> You know, Kim, that falcons are birds of prey.

Commas can be used to separate an appositive that immediately follows a noun from the rest of the sentence. An appositive is a word or phrase that explains or identifies a noun.

> Examples: Falcons, birds of prey, live on rocky cliffs. (The phrase *birds of prey* identifies and explains the noun *falcons*.)
> Some birds of prey, such as falcons, live on rocky cliffs. (The phrase *such as falcons* identifies the phrase *Some birds of prey*.)

A comma can be used to separate the two parts of a compound sentence.

> Example: There are about 40 species of falcons, and half of the species are found in Africa.

The proofreading mark (∧) is used to show where a word or punctuation mark needs to be inserted or added. Use the proofreading mark (∧) to show where each comma is needed in the sentences.

1. Kim let's look at this book about falcons.

2. Birds of prey such as hawks have hooked beaks and feet with claws.

3. Falcons are powerful fliers and they can swoop from great heights.

4. The American kestrel the smallest North American falcon is only 8 inches long.

5. A bird of prey the American kestrel eats insects mice lizards and other birds.

Fragments

A **fragment** is an incomplete sentence that does not express a complete thought.

       Examples: Anna and Beth went swimming. (sentence)

               Anna and Beth. (missing a predicate that tells what happened)

               Went swimming. (missing a subject that tells who)

Write *S* for each sentence and *F* for each fragment.

1. _____ Rang loudly and woke all of us!

2. _____ Down the dark tunnel and into a large cave.

3. _____ Pete and his cousin, Elmo.

4. _____ We will play a game after dinner.

5. _____ You may come along with us.

6. _____ The darts hit the board.

7. _____ Around the corner and over the bridge.

8. _____ That is my house.

9. _____ Frank ate the beans.

10. _____ A sandwich and some carrot sticks.

11. _____ She is a shy girl.

12. _____ The states of Texas, Michigan, and New York.

Run-On Sentences

When two independent clauses are written together, they create a run-on sentence. To avoid a run-on sentence, decide where the first sentence ends and the second begins. A run-on sentence can be corrected by separating it into two or more sentences.

Example: Casey is helpful he sets the table every night.
(run-on sentence)

Casey is helpful. He sets the table every night.
(corrected)

Separate each run-on sentence into two sentences. Put a punctuation mark at the end of the first sentence. Cross out the lowercase letter and write a capital letter above the first letter in the next word to begin the second sentence.

1. Raven has a new backpack it is green with many zippers.

2. Ray needs a paper clip he needs it to hold his papers.

3. Katie borrowed my pencil she plans to draw a map.

4. It is so cold the driveway is covered with ice.

5. Jane is outside she is on the swings.

6. Zack is helping Dad Elroy is helping Dad, too.

7. Keesha read that book she recommended it to the class.

8. Tori saw a baby squirrel it was at the bottom of that tree.

9. Zeke loves cinnamon rolls the ones with the nuts are his favorite.

10. Turn off the light it has been on too long.

Sentences, Fragments, and Run-Ons

> Remember, a declarative sentence tells a complete thought.
>
> A fragment does not tell a complete thought.
>
> A run-on sentence has too many thoughts. The thoughts are not punctuated correctly.

Write *S* for sentence, *F* for fragment, or *R* for run-on.

1. _____ Orangutans are rare animals.

2. _____ Live in rain forests in Borneo and Sumatra.

3. _____ They belong to the ape family along with chimpanzees and gorillas they are larger than most chimpanzees and smaller than most gorillas.

4. _____ About three to five feet tall.

5. _____ Their arms are extremely long.

6. _____ Male orangutans can weigh as much as an adult man or woman.

7. _____ Orangutans live in nests they swing from branch to branch and they do not get on the ground very often.

8. _____ They can use their feet just like hands.

9. _____ Orangutans are usually gentle and peaceful animals.

10. _____ Curious, too.

Name _____

Using *Good* and *Bad* Correctly

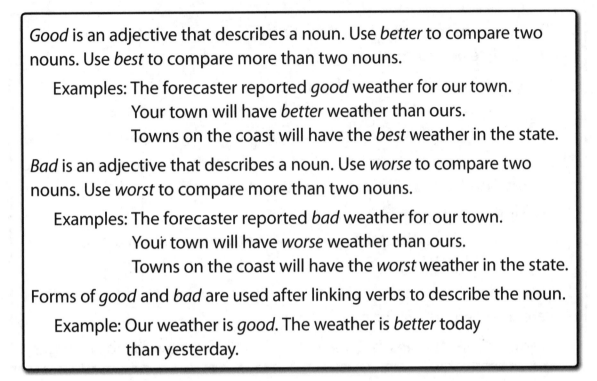

Good is an adjective that describes a noun. Use *better* to compare two nouns. Use *best* to compare more than two nouns.

Examples: The forecaster reported *good* weather for our town.
Your town will have *better* weather than ours.
Towns on the coast will have the *best* weather in the state.

Bad is an adjective that describes a noun. Use *worse* to compare two nouns. Use *worst* to compare more than two nouns.

Examples: The forecaster reported *bad* weather for our town.
Your town will have *worse* weather than ours.
Towns on the coast will have the *worst* weather in the state.

Forms of *good* and *bad* are used after linking verbs to describe the noun.

Example: Our weather is *good*. The weather is *better* today
than yesterday.

Complete each sentence with the correct form of *good* or *bad* from the parentheses.

1. The weatherperson said our weather will be _____ on Thursday than today.
(good, better, best)

2. She said the weather will be _____ over the weekend.
(good, better, best)

3. I feel _____ about that.
(good, better, best)

4. Parts of the country are having _____ storms.
(bad, worse, worst)

5. Fargo has had a _____ winter than it had last year.
(bad, worse, worst)

6. The weatherperson is predicting that the _____ snow is coming soon.
(bad, worse, worst)

7. Florida usually has _____ weather in the winter.
(good, better, best)

8. I think Florida has the _____ temperatures of all of the states.
(good, better, best)

Using *Well* and *Badly* Correctly

Well is an adverb that describes the action of a verb. Use *better* to compare two verbs. Use *best* to compare more than two verbs.

Examples: The Saturn team played *well*.
The Martian team played *better* than the Saturn team.
The Galaxy team played *best* of all of the teams.

Badly is an adverb that describes the action of a verb. Use *worse* to compare two verbs. Use *worst* to compare more than two verbs.

Examples: The Saturn team played *badly*.
The Martian team played *worse* than the Saturn team.
The Galaxy team played *worst* of all of the teams.

Well is an adjective when it is used to describe someone's health. *Better* and *best* are the comparative forms.

Example: The Martians' pitcher is feeling *well* after having elbow surgery.

Complete each sentence with the correct form of *well* or *badly* from the parentheses.

1. The baseball game went _____ for the Martians right from the first inning.
   (well, better, best)

2. The first batter, Monroe, always hits _____.
   (well, better, best)

3. The Saturns' pitcher pitched _____ to Monroe, and he missed hitting the ball.
   (badly, worse, worst)

4. Monroe runs the bases _____ than most players on his team.
   (well, better, best)

5. Stanley, the second batter, usually hits even _____ than Monroe.
   (well, better, best)

6. The pitcher threw her _____ pitches to Stanley.
   (well, better, best)

7. Stanley hit the ball _____, and it flew over the fence for a two-run homer.
   (well, better, best)

8. Things went _____ for the Saturn team in the second half of the game than the first.
   (badly, worse, worst)

Compound Words

Two words can be combined to make a **compound word**.

Example: flower + bed = flowerbed

Write a compound word on the line by adding one word from the box to each given word. Use each word only once.

boat	shore	case	port	fly	bug
board	burger	crow	coat	book	time

1. scare _____

2. cook _____

3. butter _____

4. steam _____

5. suit _____

6. rain _____

7. night _____

8. cheese _____

9. sea _____

10. air _____

11. chalk _____

12. lady _____

Contractions

A **contraction** is made by joining two words to make one new word. In a contraction, one or more letters from the words that it is made of are left out. An apostrophe (') is used in place of the left-out letter or letters. Some contractions are made from a verb and the word *not*.

Examples: do not → don't

cannot → can't

will not → won't

Write each contraction as a pair of words.

1. wouldn't _____

2. haven't _____

3. aren't _____

4. doesn't _____

Write each pair of words as a contraction.

5. had not _____

6. did not _____

7. should not _____

8. has not _____

Contractions

Some contractions are made by joining a pronoun and a linking verb.

Example: I am → I'm (An apostrophe takes the place of the *a* in *am*.)

Some contractions are made by joining a pronoun with *will* or *would*.

Examples: I will → I'll (An apostrophe takes the place of the *wi* in *will*.)

I would → I'd (An apostrophe takes the place of the *woul* in *would*.)

Write each contraction as a pair of words.

1. she'll _____

2. he'd _____

3. you've _____

4. she's _____

Write each pair of words as a contraction.

5. you are _____

6. she would _____

7. they have _____

8. he will _____

Contractions

Write each word or pair of words as a contraction.

1. she will   _____

2. you are   _____

3. he would   _____

4. there is   _____

5. I am   _____

6. cannot   _____

7. they are   _____

8. should not   _____

9. what is   _____

10. they will   _____

11. we would   _____

12. we are   _____

Name _____

Contractions

Complete the story by writing the correct contraction from the box in each blank. Use each contraction only once.

can't	can't	She'll	they're
we'll	it'll	won't	we've
it's	I've	we're	won't

I am happy because _____ my mother's birthday today. I am really excited because my father

and _____ made special plans. For weeks, _____ been planning her birthday. There is

a terrific restaurant downtown. I _____ remember its name, but _____ taking Mom

there for dinner. My grandparents _____ be able to meet us at the restaurant, but

_____ coming to our house later. That is when _____ be having cake and ice cream.

Mom _____ be expecting to see my grandparents because she thinks they are still on

vacation. There will be lots of presents for my mom to open. _____ be so surprised!

I _____ wait until tonight. I know _____ be the best birthday my mom ever had!

Using Negatives Correctly

A **negative** is a word used to make a sentence mean *no. No, no one, not, nothing, never, nobody, nowhere,* and contractions formed from a verb and *not* are examples of negative words. Only use one negative word in a sentence.

Example: I *never* have seen live flamingos.

A double negative is the incorrect use of two negative words in a sentence.

Example: I *never* have seen *no* live flamingos.

A double negative can be corrected by either removing *no* or replacing *no* with *any.*

Examples: I never have seen live flamingos.
I never have seen *any* live flamingos.

Underline the second negative in each sentence. Write a positive word on the line from the list below.

Negative	Positive	Negative	Positive
no, none	a, any, one	no one	anyone, someone
nothing	anything, something	nobody	anybody, somebody
nowhere	anywhere, somewhere	never	ever

1. There are not flamingos living nowhere near me. _____

2. Can't nobody tell me where they live? _____

3. There are not no other wading birds as big and colorful. _____

4. I never saw none other birds stand on one leg like flamingos. _____

5. There must not be nothing else like flamingos. _____

Synonyms

> **Synonyms** are words that have almost the same meaning.
>
> Examples: tired = weary
> scared = frightened

Complete each sentence with a word from the box that is a synonym for the underlined word. Use each word only once.

silent	tip	lid	mistake
small	happy	tug	tear

1. Dan's pencil <u>point</u> was dull, so he had to sharpen the _____.

2. The <u>top</u> came off the ant farm, but I quickly replaced the _____.

3. The <u>cheerful</u> girl was very _____ the day she made an A on her science project.

4. Ann got a <u>rip</u> in her jeans, so her mother repaired the _____.

5. Gina had to <u>pull</u> and _____ the heavy chair to move it.

6. Dana was <u>quiet</u> because her mother asked her to be _____ while the baby slept.

7. I made an <u>error</u>, and the teacher showed me my _____.

8. The <u>tiny</u> earring was hard to find because it was so _____.

Synonyms

Complete each sentence with a synonym for the word in parentheses. Refer to a thesaurus, if necessary.

1. Rascal is a _____ dog.
    (small)

2. Timmy can run _____.
    (fast)

3. Did you _____ your homework?
    (complete)

4. I like to _____ when I am outside.
    (yell)

5. That box is an _____ color.
    (odd)

6. Will your mother _____ us to eat pizza?
    (allow)

7. My father brought me a _____.
    (gift)

8. Kelly is wearing a _____ dress.
    (pretty)

9. Sonja recycled her _____ letters.
    (ancient)

10. The cat slept _____ the table.
    (below)

11. Patty likes to _____ with her friends.
    (chat)

12. I went on a _____ with my parents.
    (journey)

13. We had to _____ our plans when Sara broke her arm.
    (amend)

14. I would like to _____ a new coat for winter.
    (purchase)

15. Please _____ a partner for the next dance.
    (select)

Antonyms

Antonyms are words that mean the opposite of another word.

Example: hot ≠ cold

Complete the crossword puzzle using opposites from the Antonym List.

ANTONYM LIST

after	sell	late	bottom	close	weak
empty	asleep	clean	thin	quiet	different
wet	sour	subtract	pardon		

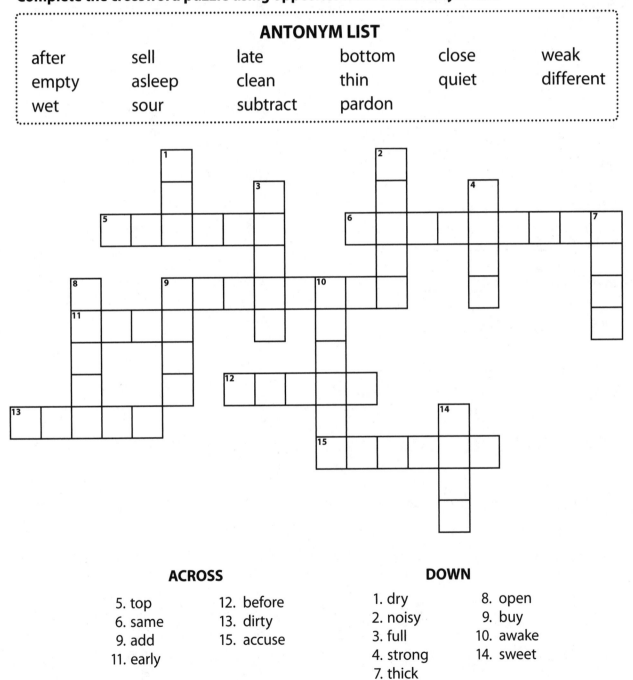

ACROSS

5. top
6. same
9. add
11. early
12. before
13. dirty
15. accuse

DOWN

1. dry
2. noisy
3. full
4. strong
7. thick
8. open
9. buy
10. awake
14. sweet

Antonyms

Write an antonym for each word. Refer to a thesaurus, if necessary.

1. ill   _____

2. soft   _____

3. smile   _____

4. first   _____

5. begin   _____

6. arrive   _____

7. light   _____

8. lost   _____

9. old   _____

10. over   _____

11. give   _____

12. forward   _____

13. stop   _____

14. always   _____

Homophones

> **Homophones** are words that are pronounced the same, but are spelled differently and have different meanings. Homophones can be confusing when you hear them.
>
> Example: The *prince prints* books. (*Prince* and *prints* sound alike, but *prince* is a male in a royal family and *prints* means "to publish" in this sentence.)

Complete each sentence with the correct homophone from the parentheses. Refer to a dictionary, if necessary.

1. The U.S. Coast Guard may use a small _____ large boat to help people in trouble in the water.   (oar, or)

2. They _____ how to stay safe when helping other people.
   (know, no)

3. Rescuers _____ small boats close to shore.
   (ewes, use)

4. Large boats have powerful radios and equipment _____ navigation.
   (for, four)

5. They have first aid kits and survival gear on _____ their boats.
   (board, bored)

6. The Coast Guard can _____ a ship to shore.
   (toe, tow)

7. Rescues at _____ are often difficult.
   (sea, see)

8. For example, last year a _____ sailor was in trouble.
   (loan, lone)

9. The Coast Guard raced to the _____ in a helicopter.
   (scene, seen)

10. Choose five homophones you did not use as correct answers in the sentences above. On another sheet of paper, write a sentence for each one. Refer to a dictionary, if necessary.

Prefixes

A **prefix** is a group of letters added to the beginning of a word. A prefix adds meaning or changes the word's meaning. The word to which the prefix is added is called the root word or base word. When adding a prefix, the spelling of the root word is not changed.

Some common prefixes and their meanings are:

re: again   pre: before   un, dis, mis: not or against   bi: two   uni: one

Draw a line from each word to its correct meaning.

1. unhappy   view again

2. bicycle   not known

3. review   every two months

4. uncover   cycle with one wheel

5. unlimited   not happy

6. prewritten   not cover

7. bimonthly   not limited

8. unknown   cycle with two wheels

9. unicycle   written before

Underline the word with a prefix in each sentence. Write the meaning of the word on the line.

10. Anabelle's umbrella stayed unopened until it began to rain. _____

11. Cicily bought prewashed jeans. _____

12. Sam is going for his biweekly allergy shot. _____

Prefixes

Use the Prefix List and Root Word List to create as many words as you can. Use another sheet of paper if necessary.

PREFIX LIST

dis   in   pre   re   un

ROOT WORD LIST

able	miss	charge	heat	fill	wind
form	capable	qualify	cover	pay	close
related	view				

1. _____

2. _____

3. _____

4. _____

5. _____

6. _____

7. _____

8. _____

9. _____

10. _____

11. _____

12. _____

13. _____

14. _____

15. _____

16. _____

17. _____

18. _____

19. _____

20. _____

21. _____

22. _____

Suffixes

A **suffix** is a group of letters added to the end of a word. It adds meaning or changes a word's meaning. The word to which the suffix is added is called the root word or base word. When a suffix begins with a consonant, changes to the base word usually are not needed.

Some common suffixes beginning with consonants are *ful, ly, less,* and *ness.*

Combine each base word and suffix to make a word with a suffix.

1. pain + ful = _____

2. forget + ful = _____

3. forgive + ness = _____

4. cheer + ful + ly = _____

5. sincere + ly = _____

6. near + ly = _____

7. fear + less = _____

8. hair + less = _____

9. care + less = _____

10. grace + ful = _____

11. sad + ness = _____

12. glad + ness = _____

Suffixes

Remember, the word to which the suffix is added is called the root word or base word.

When a root word ends in a vowel plus *y*, the root word usually does not change.

Example: play ⟶ playful, player

When a root word ends in a consonant plus *y*, change the *y* to *i* before adding the suffix.

Example: happy ⟶ happiness, happily

Some common suffixes beginning with consonants are *ful, ly, less,* and *ness*.

Use the Suffix List and Root Word List to create as many words as you can. Use another sheet of paper if necessary.

SUFFIX LIST				
er	ful	less	ly	ness

ROOT WORD LIST				
teach	wonder	awkward	thought	bake
help	beauty	play	peace	boast
care	law	wonder	doubt	quick
quiet	shy	friend		

1. _____

2. _____

3. _____

4. _____

5. _____

6. _____

7. _____

8. _____

9. _____

10. _____

11. _____

12. _____

13. _____

14. _____

15. _____

16. _____

17. _____

18. _____

Root Words

Write the root word of each word.

1. playful _____

2. rewrite _____

3. spoonful _____

4. happiness _____

5. kindness _____

6. dismiss _____

7. uncover _____

8. quickly _____

9. fearless _____

10. pretest _____

11. helpless _____

12. cleanness _____

13. incomplete _____

14. sadly _____

Capitalization

> Remember, use capital letters for the first word in a sentence, proper nouns, the pronoun *I*, and important words in book and movie titles.

Circle the letters that need to be capitalized.

1. she played ball on our team.

2. dr. jones is our dentist.

3. do you know paul brown?

4. we are going to atlanta this summer.

5. mr. green and mr. smith are good friends.

6. may we go to the park on sunday?

7. on tuesday, we can go swimming.

8. my mom gets two weeks off from work in december.

9. are you going with us on wednesday?

10. please call robin stuart tonight.

11. we are traveling to california on friday.

12. have you met my friend maria?

13. marsha and matthew are sister and brother.

14. our teacher this year is mr. perry.

Capitalization

Each sentence has one or more capitalization mistakes. Write each sentence correctly on the line below.

1. laura ingalls wilder wrote the book little house on the prairie.

   _____

2. my friend shelly moved to pennsylvania.

   _____

3. i will go visit grandma hazel next summer.

   _____

4. last saturday, we went to see the movie the lost treasure.

   _____

5. our neighbor, mr. johnson, lets us fish in his pond.

   _____

6. I like to shop at saunders shoes at the mall.

   _____

7. we named our new kitten muffin.

   _____

8. we always go to the fair in september.

   _____

Capitalization

> Capitalize the first letter of a person's first and last name.
>
> Examples: I spoke with *Tommy* today.
> She gave *Nancy Connor* a gift.
>
> Capitalize a personal title when it is in front of a person's name.
>
> Example: *President* Patricia Garcia and *Mr.* Hank Parker are coming to dinner.

Cross out each word in the paragraph that needs a capital letter. Write the word with the correct capital letter in the space above the crossed-out word.

pocahontas was a Native American who lived in Virginia during the time of the first English settlement.

According to legend, pocahontas saved the life of captain john smith. Later, she moved into

Jamestown and took the name rebecca. She married mr. john rolfe, and they traveled to England to

meet king james. pocahontas died in England and was buried there. She had one son, thomas.

Name _____

Capitalization

> Capitalize the names of geographical places, such as cities, states, countries, and continents.
>
> > Example: *California* is in the *United States*, on the continent of *North America*.
>
> Capitalize the names of important man-made places.
>
> > Example: They went to see the *Statue of Liberty*.

Circle each geographical name that needs a capital letter.

1. Famous for its golden gate bridge, san francisco lies by the pacific ocean.

2. Famous for its french quarter, new orleans is the last port on the mississippi river.

3. Famous for its liberty bell, philadelphia is in the state of pennsylvania.

4. Famous for tea, rice, and silk, china is the home of the great wall.

5. Famous for its pasta, grapes, and gondolas, italy is the home of the roman coliseum.

6. Famous for safaris and large game preserves, kenya is bordered on the west by lake victoria.

Rewrite two of the sentences above, using correct capitalization.

7. _____

_____

8. _____

_____

Name _____

Parts of a Letter

Letters have five parts: **date, greeting, body, closing,** and **signature**. Capitalize the first word in greetings and closings. Greetings and closings end with commas. The greeting, closing, and signature have their own lines.

Example:

January 2, 2009

Dear Grandpa,

Thank you for taking me fishing. I liked catching all of those fish. They tasted great for dinner. I hope we catch more when we go fishing again.

Love,

Tricia

Fill in the missing parts of these letters. Label each part.

1.

Dear Mike,
You are invited to my house for my birthday party. Please let me know if you can come.

Sincerely,

2.

I went to the library on Monday. I chose five books and listened to a great storyteller.
I hope you can meet me there next Monday.

Parts of a Letter

Remember, when writing a letter, capitalize the first word in the greeting.

Example: Dear neighbor,

Also, capitalize the first word of the closing.

Examples: Yours truly, Sincerely, Your friend,

1. Circle all of the words below that need capital letters.

july 1, 2008

dear Aunt Laura,

Thank you so much for the gift card. I am going to use it to buy a game I have been wanting. When you and Uncle Mike come to visit this summer, we can all play my new game.

your nephew,

Mickey

2. Fill in the blanks below using correct capitalization.

(date) _____

(greeting) _____,

It was wonderful to see you last week. I'm so glad you could come for a visit. I especially enjoyed our trip to the Science Center. On your next visit, we can go to the museum in town. I hope to see you again soon.

(closing) _____,

Dianne

Friendly Letters and Business Letters

Friendly letters and **business letters** differ in their purposes, but the same capitalization rules apply to both types of letters. In addition to the five parts of a friendly letter—the date, the greeting, the body, the closing, and the signature—a business letter has an inside address.

Example of a greeting for a friendly letter: Dear Mom and Dad,

Example of a greeting for a business letter: Dear Toy Palace:

Example of a closing for a friendly and a business letter: Sincerely,

1. Circle each letter that should be capitalized in the friendly letter.

august 1, 2008

dear barbara,

i am really enjoying my summer vacation on my uncle's ranch. there are horses to ride, and my cousins and i go fishing every day. i'll see you in two more weeks, and then i can show you my pictures.

your friend,

bonnie

2. Circle each letter that should be capitalized in the business letter.

4407 ninth street
hillside, maine 04024

march 10, 2008

skateboards and more
6243 rock ave.
detroit, michigan 48201

To whom it may concern:

I am returning my skateboard for repair. it is still under warranty. please repair it and return the skateboard to the address above as soon as possible.

sincerely,

sam smith

Commas in Letters

When writing a date, use a **comma** (,) to separate the day from the year.
   Example: October 6, 2000

Use an additional comma after the year if it is not the last word in a sentence.
   Example: October 6, 2000, was the date on which Julia was born.

Use a comma to separate the name of a city from the state.
   Example: Toledo, Ohio

Use an additional comma after the name of the state if it is not the last word in a sentence.
   Example: Toledo, Ohio, was Julia's birthplace.

Use a comma after the greeting and after the closing of both a friendly letter and a business letter:
   Examples: Dear Julia, (greeting) Sincerely, (closing)

Write commas in each phrase or sentence where they belong.

1. My family visits Spring Grove Minnesota every year in the summer. _____

   _____

2. Dear Grandpa _____

3. Yours truly _____

4. On October 9 2008 Carolyn saw the play. _____

5. My aunt and uncle live in North Branch New York. _____

   _____

6. Dear Jon _____

7. January 1 2009 _____

8. Paris Texas is located in the northeast part of the state. _____

   _____

Name _____

Writing Letters

Write a friendly letter.

_____

_____

_____

_____

_____

_____

_____

_____

_____

Write a business letter.

_____

_____

_____

_____

_____

_____

_____

_____

_____

_____

103

Name _____

Common Nouns

A **common noun** is a word that names a person, place, or thing.
Examples: child (person), school (place), book (thing)

Underline each noun that names a person.

<u>boy</u>	<u>friend</u>	<u>student</u>
<u>coach</u>	<u>secretary</u>	game
both	jolly	<u>teacher</u>
house	<u>sister</u>	<u>actor</u>

Underline each noun that names a place.

<u>science lab</u>	<u>classroom</u>	food
<u>playground</u>	<u>hallway</u>	<u>clinic</u>
sun	paper	<u>office</u>
<u>park</u>	dog	<u>diner</u>

Underline each noun that names a thing.

<u>desk</u>	<u>dictionary</u>	<u>ruler</u>
neighbor	<u>lunch box</u>	city
house	<u>window</u>	<u>book</u>
<u>truck</u>	<u>banana</u>	teacher

Name _____

Common Nouns

Complete each sentence by writing a noun that makes sense in each blank.

1. The _____ drove his _____ through the field.
2. The _____ went to the beach.
3. A nurse works in a _____.
4. The _____ blew in the wind.
5. My mom put a _____ in a jar.
6. The _____ belongs to _____.
7. A _____ tastes sweet.
8. The _____ broke down in the _____.
9. Taylor walked with his _____ to the _____.
10. Juan took a _____ to the park.
11. The _____ fell off the tree.
12. I always eat my snack in the _____.

Answers will vary.

Name _____

Proper Nouns

A **proper noun** is the name of a specific person, place, or thing.
Begin all proper nouns with a capital letter.
Example: *Todd* took pictures of *Lookout Mountain* in *Tennessee*.

Underline the proper nouns in each sentence below.

1. The official address of the president of the <u>United States</u> is 1600 <u>Pennsylvania Avenue</u>.
2. The house at 1600 Pennsylvania Avenue used to be called the <u>President's House</u>.
3. The first president of the United States, <u>George Washington</u>, did not live in the <u>President's House</u>.
4. <u>John Adams</u> and his wife, <u>Abigail</u>, were the first to live there.
5. Soldiers from <u>Great Britain</u> burned the <u>President's House</u> during the <u>War of 1812</u>, so <u>President Monroe</u> lived near <u>20th Street</u> for nine months.
6. <u>Andrew Jackson</u> had magnolia trees planted on the south lawn, called <u>President's Park</u>.
7. <u>President Teddy Roosevelt</u> changed the name of the house to the <u>White House</u> in 1901.
8. There was a second fire in the <u>West Wing</u> of the <u>White House</u> in 1929, while <u>Herbert Hoover</u> was president.
9. The inside of the <u>White House</u> was remodeled throughout much of <u>President Harry S. Truman's</u> term, so his family lived across <u>Pennsylvania Avenue</u> in the <u>Blair House</u>.
10. Another name for the <u>White House</u> is the <u>Executive Mansion</u>.

Name _____

Proper Nouns

Circle the proper nouns in each sentence that need to begin with a capital letter.

1. My friends, (jim) and (marty,) want to join the (boy scouts.)
2. I heard (ms. smith's) class visited the (lincoln memorial) in (washington, d.c.)
3. Does your cousin (mary) go to (winn school?)
4. When his family was in (idaho), (mike) floated down the (snake river.)
5. Last night, (doug) stopped at the (brookstown mall) to buy a gift.
6. Have you visited (niagara falls) in (new york?)
7. Yesterday, (dana) and her sister (meg) attended a party at the (natural science museum.)
8. When did (avery) and (raul) watch the baseball game at (bryant stadium?)

Write two sentences about specific places you have visited.

9. _____ **Answers will vary.** _____

10. _____

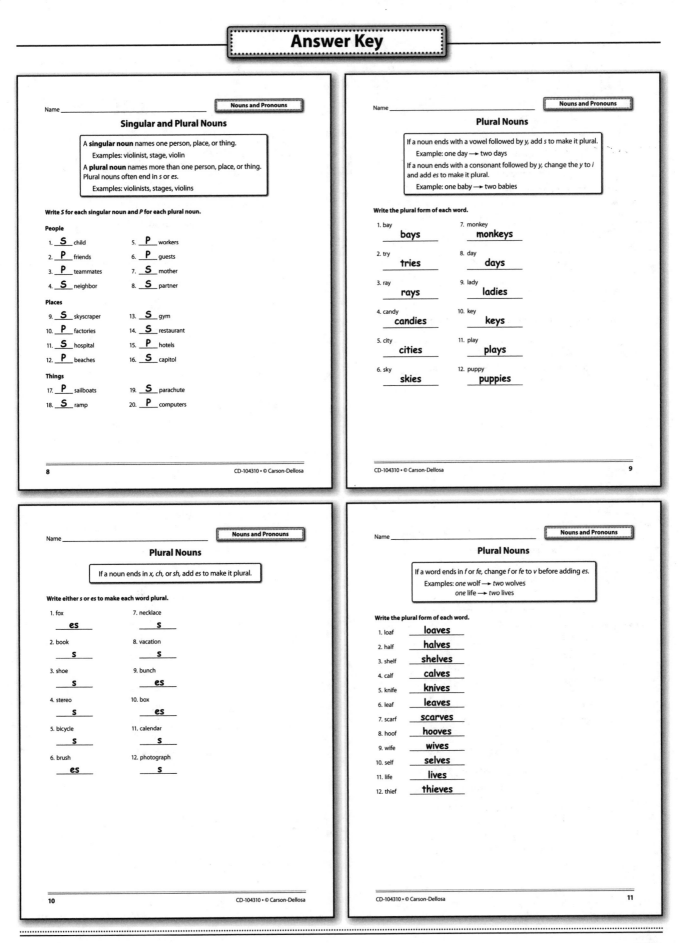

Page 8 — Singular and Plural Nouns

A **singular noun** names one person, place, or thing.
Examples: violinist, stage, violin
A **plural noun** names more than one person, place, or thing. Plural nouns often end in s or es.
Examples: violinists, stages, violins

Write S for each singular noun and P for each plural noun.

People
1. S child
2. P friends
3. P teammates
4. S neighbor
5. P workers
6. P guests
7. S mother
8. S partner

Places
9. S skyscraper
10. P factories
11. S hospital
12. P beaches
13. S gym
14. S restaurant
15. P hotels
16. S capitol

Things
17. P sailboats
18. S ramp
19. S parachute
20. P computers

Page 9 — Plural Nouns

If a noun ends with a vowel followed by y, add s to make it plural.
Example: one day → two days
If a noun ends with a consonant followed by y, change the y to i and add es to make it plural.
Example: one baby → two babies

Write the plural form of each word.
1. bay — bays
2. try — tries
3. ray — rays
4. candy — candies
5. city — cities
6. sky — skies
7. monkey — monkeys
8. day — days
9. lady — ladies
10. key — keys
11. play — plays
12. puppy — puppies

Page 10 — Plural Nouns

If a noun ends in x, ch, or sh, add es to make it plural.

Write either s or es to make each word plural.
1. fox — es
2. book — s
3. shoe — s
4. stereo — s
5. bicycle — s
6. brush — es
7. necklace — s
8. vacation — s
9. bunch — es
10. box — es
11. calendar — s
12. photograph — s

Page 11 — Plural Nouns

If a word ends in f or fe, change f or fe to v before adding es.
Examples: one wolf → two wolves
one life → two lives

Write the plural form of each word.
1. loaf — loaves
2. half — halves
3. shelf — shelves
4. calf — calves
5. knife — knives
6. leaf — leaves
7. scarf — scarves
8. hoof — hooves
9. wife — wives
10. self — selves
11. life — lives
12. thief — thieves

Irregular Plural Nouns

Some nouns have irregular plural forms.
Examples: man → men
moose → moose

Draw a line to match each singular noun to its irregular plural form.

Singular	Plural	Singular	Plural
1. cactus	feet	5. child	mice
2. deer	deer	6. goose	women
3. foot	oxen	7. mouse	children
4. ox	cacti	8. woman	geese

Rewrite each sentence with the plural form of each underlined noun.

9. The man chased the ox down the road.

The men chased the oxen down the road.

10. The woman and the child fed the goose.

The women and the children fed the geese.

12

Possessive Nouns

A **singular possessive noun** shows ownership by one person or thing. To make a singular possessive noun, add an apostrophe plus s ('s) to the end of a singular noun.
Examples: cat's claws
boy's jacket
Bill's book

A **plural possessive noun** shows ownership by more than one person or thing. To make a plural possessive noun, add an apostrophe (') to the end of a plural noun.
Examples: dogs' ears
cars' tires
kids' toys

Circle the possessive noun in each sentence. Then, circle S if the possessive noun is singular or P if the possessive noun is plural.

1. (Mary's) pet bird knows 12 words. (S) P
2. The (girls) dresses were all very pretty. S (P)
3. Many of the (stadium's) seats needed painting. (S) P
4. Why were the (books') pages ripped out? S (P)

Write apostrophes in the correct places in each sentence.

5. Did Jim's dad talk to the team's coaches?
6. Some of the ladies' golf clubs were bent or broken.
7. The skier's helmet was red and white.
8. Grant's baseball glove was left in Matt's car.

13

Possessive Nouns

For irregular nouns with plural forms that do not end in s, add apostrophe plus s ('s) to make the noun possessive.
Examples: children's mittens
mice's tails

Write the plural possessive form of each noun.

1. officer	officer's	5. frames	frames'
2. people	people's	6. moose	moose's
3. men	men's	7. reptiles	reptiles'
4. berries	berries'	8. courses	courses'

Write each phrase below using a possessive noun for each underlined noun.

Example: the room of the boys → the boys' room

9. the dance of the ballerinas — the ballerinas' dance
10. the taste of the cookies — the cookies' taste
11. the meeting of the women — the women's meeting
12. the playground of the children — the children's playground

14

Possessive Nouns

Write the possessive form of each underlined word.

1. That is Danas dollhouse. — Dana's
2. Craigs truck is big. — Craig's
3. I like Sharons new green bicycle. — Sharon's
4. The childrens song was sung perfectly. — children's
5. The two girls kites flew high in the sky. — girls'
6. The schools end-of-the-year picnic was fun. — school's
7. The trains loud whistle scared Barbara. — train's
8. The actors costume was colorful. — actor's
9. I love to visit my grandmothers house. — grandmother's
10. The singers voices are lovely. — singers'
11. The dogs collars are green. — dogs'
12. Omar walked to his neighborhoods park. — neighborhood's

15

Name _____ **Nouns and Pronouns**

Possessive Nouns

Example: Grandmothers glasses _____.
→ Grandmother's glasses fell off the chair.

Write an apostrophe in the correct place in each underlined word. Then, complete each sentence.

1. A dolphin's fin _____ **Sentences will vary.**
2. Janet's dimples _____
3. The roses' stems _____
4. That car's wheels _____
5. Two robots' eyes _____
6. Kenny's bike _____
7. Linda's doll _____
8. Maria's son _____
9. Ten girls' stickers _____
10. Her three kittens' toys _____

16   CD-104310 • © Carson-Dellosa

Name _____ **Nouns and Pronouns**

Pronouns

A **pronoun** is a word that takes the place of a noun. *I, you, he, she, we, they, me, him, her, it, us,* and *them* are examples of pronouns.

Write the correct pronoun from the parentheses to complete each sentence.

1. Tia and **I** took the newspapers to the recycling center. (me, I)
2. Mark went to the store with **me**. (me, I)
3. Bruce is going to Grandfather's farm next summer to visit **him**. (he, him)
4. Do you have any coins you could give **us** for our collection? (us, we)
5. Lisa and Barry mowed the yard, so Dad gave **them** $3.00 each. (they, them)
6. Beto said **he** would meet us at the game. (he, him)
7. Maria realized she was late when **she** glanced at the clock. (she, her)
8. When **we** make hot chocolate, the water must be very hot. (us, we)
9. **They** took us to the basketball game after school. (They, Them)
10. Mom drove **her** dog to the veterinarian's office. (she, her)

CD-104310 • © Carson-Dellosa   17

Name _____ **Nouns and Pronouns**

Subject Pronouns

A **subject pronoun** is a word that can be used to replace the subject of a sentence. The subject of a sentence tells who or what the sentence is about. *You, I, he, she, it, we,* and *they* are examples of subject pronouns.
You and *I* can be used as the subject of a sentence.

Example: *You* and *I* enjoy watching bicycle races.

He, she, it, we, and *they* can replace nouns and phrases containing nouns in the subject part of a sentence.

Example: The Tour de France is a bicycle race. → *It* is a bicycle race.

Write the correct subject pronoun to replace each word or group of words.

1. scientists **they**   4. the girl **she**
2. Mr. Keller **he**   5. our class **we**
3. mouth **it**

Rewrite each sentence. Replace each underlined word with the correct subject pronoun from the box.

| they | he | she | it | we |

6. Ms. Keller and her husband are marine biologists.
She and her husband are marine biologists.
7. My class heard them speak about squids.
We heard them speak about squids.
8. Giant squids live in the ocean.
They live in the ocean.

18   CD-104310 • © Carson-Dellosa

Name _____ **Nouns and Pronouns**

Object Pronouns

An **object pronoun** is a word that can replace a noun or a phrase in the predicate of a sentence. The predicate of a sentence is the part that includes the verb. An object pronoun receives the action of the verb. *Him, her, it, us,* and *them* are examples of object pronouns.
Example: Thunderstorms frighten my brother. → Thunderstorms frighten *him.*

Write the correct object pronoun to replace each word or group of words.

| him | her | it | us | them |

1. Carlos **him**   5. clouds **them**
2. Lisa **her**   6. water **it**
3. rain **it**   7. Jack and me **us**
4. lightning **it**   8. sound waves **them**

Rewrite each sentence. Replace each underlined word with the correct object pronoun from the box.

9. Mother called Carlos and me to come inside the house.
Mother called us to come inside the house.
10. Big, black clouds mean a thunderstorm is coming.
Big, black clouds mean it is coming.
11. We see flashes of lightning in the clouds.
We see flashes of lightning in them.

CD-104310 • © Carson-Dellosa   19

Name _____

Nouns and Pronouns

Object Pronouns

Read each pair of sentences. Complete the second sentence with the correct object pronoun.

1. Lisa received paint as a gift.

   Lisa received _____**it**_____ as a gift.

2. She painted four pictures of Lucy and me.

   She painted four pictures of _____**us**_____.

3. In one picture, she showed Lucy riding a bike.

   In one picture, she showed _____**her**_____ riding a bike.

4. Then, she painted a picture of her dog and cat.

   Then, she painted a picture of _____**them**_____.

5. Lisa hung her pictures up to dry.

   Lisa hung _____**them**_____ up to dry.

6. She asked her mom and me to look at the pictures.

   She asked _____**us**_____ to look at the pictures.

7. We liked the picture of the dog and cat best.

   We liked the picture of _____**them**_____ best.

8. Lisa's mom hung the picture on the refrigerator.

   Lisa's mom hung _____**it**_____ on the refrigerator.

20 CD-104310 • © Carson-Dellosa

Name _____

Nouns and Pronouns

Subject and Object Pronouns

Write a sentence for each pronoun in the box.

| he | me | us | she | him | you | it | her |

1. **Answers will vary.**
2.
3.
4.
5.
6.
7.
8.

CD-104310 • © Carson-Dellosa 21

Name _____

Nouns and Pronouns

Possessive Pronouns

A **possessive pronoun** tells who or what has something or owns something. *His, her, my, your, our, their,* and *its* are examples of possessive pronouns.

Example: Betsy Griscom's family lived in Philadelphia. → *Her* family lived in Philadelphia.

Read each pair of sentences. Complete the second sentence with the correct possessive pronoun.

1. Betsy Griscom is a person from history.

   _____**Her**_____ family is known for living in a simple and peaceful way.

2. Betsy's parents had 17 children.

   They taught _____**their**_____ children to help with the chores.

3. In 1773, Betsy married John Ross.

   _____**His**_____ job was to cover furniture with fabric, so Betsy sewed a lot to help him.

4. General George Washington designed a flag for the colonies.

   He gave _____**his**_____ sketch to Betsy Griscom Ross to sew.

5. Betsy created the first American flag.

   The flag served as a symbol of freedom to _____**its**_____ citizens.

6. Today, the American flag has 50 stars, one for each state.

   _____**Its**_____ colors are red, white, and blue.

22 CD-104310 • © Carson-Dellosa

Name _____

Nouns and Pronouns

Possessive Pronouns

Write the possessive form of each underlined word.

1. Mary's science report was about aardvarks. — **Her**
2. Aardvarks' appearance may look strange to us. — **Their**
3. Aardvarks' bodies are arched, and they have long noses. — **Their**
4. An aardvark's ears are large, and an aardvark's tail is long. — **Its, its**
5. An aardvark's diet consists mostly of insects. — **Its**
6. An aardvark's claws are powerful. — **Its**
7. A baby aardvark's mother looks after the baby for about a year. — **Its**
8. Mary's next science report will be on anteaters. — **Her**

CD-104310 • © Carson-Dellosa 23

Name _____   Nouns and Pronouns

Possessive Pronouns

These possessive pronouns come before nouns and show ownership: *my, his, her, its, our, your,* and *their.*

Example: John's car is red. → *His* car is red.

These possessive pronouns also can be used alone: *his, hers, its.*

Example: That is Anne's doll. → That is *hers.*

These possessive pronouns are always used alone: *mine, ours, yours,* and *theirs.*

Example: That is my basketball. → That is *mine.*

Read each pair of sentences. Complete the second sentence with the correct possessive pronoun.

1. Mrs. Atkins is the children's teacher.

   Mrs. Atkins is **their** teacher.

2. Mrs. Atkins's hair is red.

   Her hair is red.

3. The desk next to the pencil sharpener is Mario's.

   It is **his**.

4. Paul put his lunch box on the table.

   "This lunch box is **mine**," he said.

5. It is Ingrid and Juan's responsibility to keep the bookshelves neat.

   The responsibility is **theirs**.

6. "We like this classroom," said the children.

   "It is **our** classroom," they said.

24   CD-104310 • © Carson-Dellosa

Name _____   Verbs

Action Verbs

An **action verb** tells what someone or something is doing.

Examples: The boy *swings* the golf club.
The mouse *scampers* across the floor.

Circle the action verb in each sentence.

1. Waldo (hides) from his friend.
2. James (dashes) behind the tree.
3. Marshall (searches) for the others.
4. Helen (sits) under the swing.
5. Jane (kneels) behind the slide.
6. Sam (crawls) along the fence.
7. Marshall (finds) Karen.
8. Karen (races) for the free spot.
9. Marshall (tags) Karen.
10. Karen (calls) for everyone to come out.

CD-104310 • © Carson-Dellosa   25

Name _____   Verbs

Action Verbs

Write an action verb that makes sense in each phrase.

Answers will vary.

1. _____ three fish
2. _____ for a clue
3. _____ a fun game
4. _____ the ball
5. _____ the milk
6. _____ the bike
7. _____ four cookies
8. _____ through the magnifying glass
9. _____ a question
10. _____ a log cabin
11. _____ the baseball game
12. _____ the flower seeds
13. _____ the picture
14. _____ in the pool
15. _____ a new coat
16. _____ the buttons
17. _____ the apple
18. _____ the red wagon
19. _____ a good story
20. _____ a pretty picture

26   CD-104310 • © Carson-Dellosa

Name _____   Verbs

Present Tense Action Verbs

A **present tense action verb** shows action that is happening now. When the noun in the subject of a sentence is singular, present tense action verbs often end in *s* or *es.*

Example: Stuart *reads* a book about a starfish.

Write the present tense action verb from the parentheses to complete each sentence.

1. A starfish **lives** in the sea.
   (lived, lives)

2. It **forms** one five-pointed star with its arms.
   (forms, formed)

3. Its arms **stretch** one foot across.
   (stretches, stretch)

4. If the starfish **injures** an arm, it grows a new one!
   (injured, injures)

5. The starfish **crawls** along the bottom of the sea.
   (crawled, crawls)

6. It **moves** on little tube feet on its underside.
   (moved, moves)

7. The starfish **searches** for something to eat.
   (searches, searched)

8. It **spies** some tasty fish.
   (spies, spied)

CD-104310 • © Carson-Dellosa   27

Past Tense Action Verbs

Name _____

Verbs

A **past tense action verb** shows action that has already happened. The past tense of most action verbs is made by adding *ed* to the present tense verb.

Example: help → helped

Write the past tense of the underlined word in each sentence.

1. I need new shoes. — **needed**
2. The shoes at the store look comfortable. — **looked**
3. I pick the tennis shoes. — **picked**
4. I walk in them. — **walked**
5. My sister wants to borrow them. — **wanted**
6. She attempts to put them on her feet. — **attempted**
7. They squash her toes. — **squashed**

Complete each sentence. Use at least one past tense action verb in each sentence.

8. Last night, I _____.

9. This morning, I _____.

10. I _____ last week.

11. I _____ before I went to school.

12. Sam _____ us cookies at lunch.

Answers will vary.

28 CD-104310 • © Carson-Dellosa

Past Tense Action Verbs

Name _____

Verbs

Remember, most past tense action verbs are made by adding *ed* to the present tense verb.

Example: help → helped

If the verb ends in a silent *e*, drop the *e* and add *ed*.

Example: like → liked

If the verb ends with a single consonant after a single vowel, double the consonant and add *ed*.

Example: plan → planned

If the verb ends in a consonant and *y*, change the *y* to *i* and add *ed*.

Example: carry → carried

Write the past tense form of each underlined action verb.

1. They study at the town library. — **studied**
2. The peacocks show their beautiful feathers. — **showed**
3. The children like the music. — **liked**
4. Beavers flap their tails on the water to signal danger. — **flapped**
5. Some monkeys curl their tails around a branch. — **curled**
6. The people hurry inside before the rain started. — **hurried**
7. Mel and Vanessa stop at the crosswalk. — **stopped**
8. They wait for the school bus. — **waited**

CD-104310 • © Carson-Dellosa 29

Past Tense Action Verbs

Name _____

Verbs

Write the past tense form of each present tense verb.

Present Tense	Past Tense
1. glide	**glided**
2. invent	**invented**
3. dream	**dreamed**
4. cry	**cried**
5. spot	**spotted**
6. guess	**guessed**
7. hurry	**hurried**
8. report	**reported**

Write two sentences with past tense action verbs.

9. _____ **Answers will vary.** _____

10. _____

30 CD-104310 • © Carson-Dellosa

Past Tense Action Verbs

Name _____

Verbs

Write the past tense form of each underlined action verb.

1. A tadpole hatches from an egg in a pond. — **hatched**
2. It looks like a small fish at first. — **looked**
3. The tadpole uses its tail to swim. — **used**
4. It breathes with gills. — **breathed**
5. Its appearance changes after a few weeks. — **changed**
6. It starts to grow hind legs. — **started**
7. Its head flattens. — **flattened**
8. Its gills vanish. — **vanished**

CD-104310 • © Carson-Dellosa 31

Name _____

Future Tense Verbs

A **future tense verb** shows action that has not happened yet. It tells about action that will or may happen in the future. The future tense often includes helping verbs like *will* and *might* in front of a main verb.

Examples: We *will go* to school tomorrow.
I *might take* ballet lessons.

Write *F* in front of each sentence with a future tense verb. Then, rewrite the sentences that are not marked with *F* in the future tense.

F 1. He is coming to my house to play.

F 2. They will bring cookies to the picnic.

F 3. I will be the line leader tomorrow.

_____ 4. Terry sings with the music.

_____ 5. Billy is listening to the radio.

F 6. Jill and Nan might go to the fair next week.

Terry will sing with the music.

Billy will be listening to the radio.

_____

_____

_____

_____

CD-104310 • © Carson-Dellosa

Name _____

Future Tense Verbs

Write the future tense verb from the parentheses to complete each sentence.

1. Mary _____**will cook**_____ dinner tonight.
   (will cook, cooked)

2. Angelo _____**might visit**_____ his stepmom this weekend.
   (visit, might visit)

3. Carrie _____**might go**_____ to the movies tomorrow.
   (might go, went)

4. Scott _____**will read**_____ his new book this evening.
   (is reading, will read)

5. Wendy _____**will show**_____ me her new bracelet when she returns.
   (showed, will show)

6. You and I _____**could play**_____ in the park tomorrow.
   (could play, played)

Read each pair of sentences. Circle the sentence that shows future tense.

7. Bob ran to the market.   (Bob will run around the block.)

8. I am having green beans with dinner.   (I will have corn tomorrow.)

9. (Troy will catch the ball.)   Troy catches the ball.

10. (He may go to the new school.)   He went to the new school.

11. Davion washed the dog.   (Davion will wash the dog.)

12. (She will walk home.)   She walks home.

CD-104310 • © Carson-Dellosa

Name _____

Past, Present, and Future Tense Verbs

Remember, verb tenses tell when something is happening.

Underline the verb in each sentence. If the verb is future tense, underline both the main verb and the helping verb before it. Circle *past, present,* or *future* to show the tense of the verb.

1. Vanessa <u>signed</u> her name on the card.   (past)   present   future

2. Greg <u>will golf</u> in the tournament.   past   present   (future)

3. Megan <u>snaps</u> the links together.   past   (present)   future

4. Brant <u>climbs</u> into his bed.   past   (present)   future

5. Layne <u>will set</u> her alarm clock.   past   present   (future)

6. Kallie <u>rocked</u> her puppy to sleep.   (past)   present   future

7. Jill <u>will dip</u> the strawberries in chocolate.   past   present   (future)

8. Raymond <u>catches</u> a fish.   past   (present)   future

9. Jade <u>calculated</u> the answer.   (past)   present   future

10. Fran <u>will ace</u> the test.   past   present   (future)

11. Ava <u>writes</u> her article.   past   (present)   future

12. Mel <u>dined</u> with her guests.   (past)   present   future

CD-104310 • © Carson-Dellosa

Name _____

Irregular Verbs

Remember, most past tense verbs are formed by adding *ed* to the present tense form of the verb. The past tense of irregular verbs is not formed in this way.

Example: I *see* the red car. (present tense)
I *saw* the red car yesterday. (past tense)

Write the past tense of each irregular verb. Look up the present tense verb in a dictionary to learn the past tense, if needed.

Present Tense	Past Tense	Present Tense	Past Tense
1. write	wrote	6. teach	taught
2. draw	drew	7. find	found
3. speak	spoke	8. feel	felt
4. hold	held	9. bend	bent
5. hear	heard	10. catch	caught

Write the past tense form of each underlined word.

11. I <u>see</u> a butterfly on a flower.   saw

12. The butterfly <u>makes</u> her egg sticky.   made

13. The tiny white egg <u>sticks</u> to the leaf.   stuck

14. A small caterpillar <u>comes</u> out of the egg.   came

CD-104310 • © Carson-Dellosa

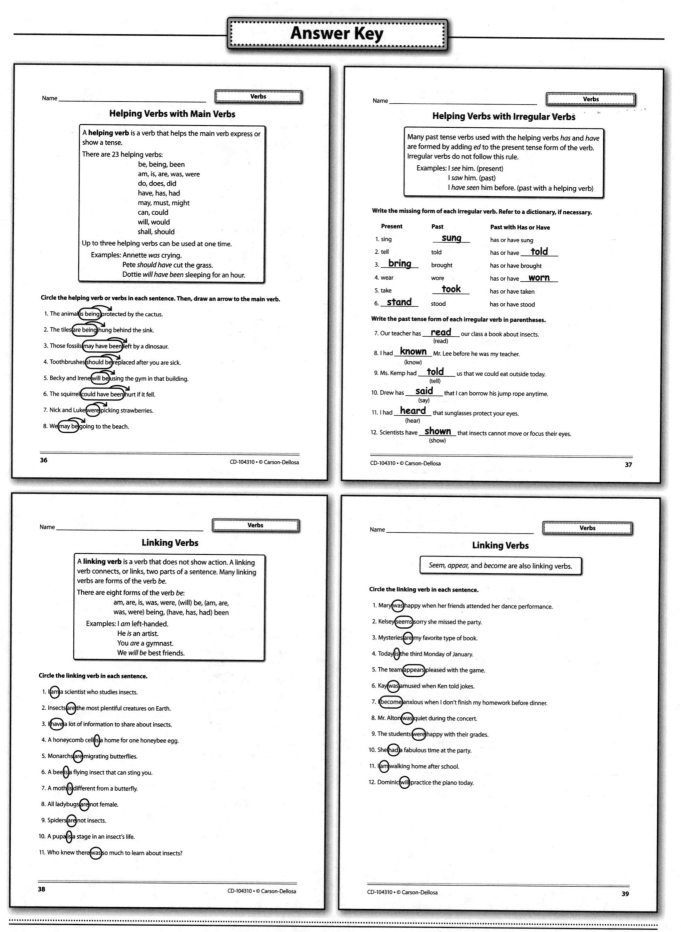

Name _____ Verbs

Helping Verbs with Main Verbs

A **helping verb** is a verb that helps the main verb express or show a tense.

There are 23 helping verbs:

be, being, been
am, is, are, was, were
do, does, did
have, has, had
may, must, might
can, could
will, would
shall, should

Up to three helping verbs can be used at one time.

Examples: Annette *was* crying.
Pete *should have* cut the grass.
Dottie *will have been* sleeping for an hour.

Circle the helping verb or verbs in each sentence. Then, draw an arrow to the main verb.

1. The animal is being protected by the cactus.
2. The tiles are being hung behind the sink.
3. Those fossils may have been left by a dinosaur.
4. Toothbrushes should be replaced after you are sick.
5. Becky and Irene will be using the gym in that building.
6. The squirrel could have been hurt if it fell.
7. Nick and Luke were picking strawberries.
8. We may be going to the beach.

36 CD-104310 • © Carson-Dellosa

Name _____ Verbs

Helping Verbs with Irregular Verbs

Many past tense verbs used with the helping verbs *has* and *have* are formed by adding *ed* to the present tense form of the verb. Irregular verbs do not follow this rule.

Examples: I *see* him. (present)
I *saw* him. (past)
I *have seen* him before. (past with a helping verb)

Write the missing form of each irregular verb. Refer to a dictionary, if necessary.

Present	Past	Past with Has or Have
1. sing	**sung**	has or have sung
2. tell	told	has or have **told**
3. **bring**	brought	has or have brought
4. wear	wore	has or have **worn**
5. take	**took**	has or have taken
6. **stand**	stood	has or have stood

Write the past tense form of each irregular verb in parentheses.

7. Our teacher has **read** our class a book about insects.
(read)
8. I had **known** Mr. Lee before he was my teacher.
(know)
9. Ms. Kemp had **told** us that we could eat outside today.
(tell)
10. Drew has **said** that I can borrow his jump rope anytime.
(say)
11. I had **heard** that sunglasses protect your eyes.
(hear)
12. Scientists have **shown** that insects cannot move or focus their eyes.
(show)

CD-104310 • © Carson-Dellosa 37

Name _____ Verbs

Linking Verbs

A **linking verb** is a verb that does not show action. A linking verb connects, or links, two parts of a sentence. Many linking verbs are forms of the verb *be*.

There are eight forms of the verb *be*:

am, are, is, was, were, (will) be, (am, are, was, were) being, (have, has, had) been

Examples: I *am* left-handed.
He *is* an artist.
You *are* a gymnast.
We *will be* best friends.

Circle the linking verb in each sentence.

1. I am a scientist who studies insects.
2. Insects are the most plentiful creatures on Earth.
3. I have a lot of information to share about insects.
4. A honeycomb cell is a home for one honeybee egg.
5. Monarchs are migrating butterflies.
6. A bee is a flying insect that can sting you.
7. A moth is different from a butterfly.
8. All ladybugs are not female.
9. Spiders are not insects.
10. A pupa is a stage in an insect's life.
11. Who knew there was so much to learn about insects?

38 CD-104310 • © Carson-Dellosa

Name _____ Verbs

Linking Verbs

Seem, appear, and *become* are also linking verbs.

Circle the linking verb in each sentence.

1. Mary was happy when her friends attended her dance performance.
2. Kelsey seems sorry she missed the party.
3. Mysteries are my favorite type of book.
4. Today is the third Monday of January.
5. The team appears pleased with the game.
6. Kay was amused when Ken told jokes.
7. I become anxious when I don't finish my homework before dinner.
8. Mr. Alton was quiet during the concert.
9. The students were happy with their grades.
10. She had a fabulous time at the party.
11. I am walking home after school.
12. Dominic will practice the piano today.

CD-104310 • © Carson-Dellosa 39

Answer Key

Present Tense Action Verbs and Linking Verbs (Page 40)

Remember, a present tense action verb shows action that is happening now. Present tense action verbs end in *s* or *es* when the noun in the subject is singular.

Example: It jumps.

Also remember, a linking verb does not show action. It links two parts of a sentence.

Example: It *is* funny.

Write A for each present tense action verb and L for each linking verb.

1. bloom **A**
2. scream **A**
3. seems **L**
4. has **L**
5. have **L**
6. pretend **A**
7. becomes **L**
8. walk **A**
9. were **L**
10. skip **A**
11. appears **L**
12. hatch **A**
13. is **L**
14. stir **A**
15. study **A**
16. hold **A**
17. am **L**
18. was **L**
19. jump **A**
20. scatter **A**

40   CD-104310 • © Carson-Dellosa

Present Tense Action Verbs and Linking Verbs (Page 41)

Write the correct present tense action or linking verb from the parentheses to complete each sentence.

1. The jumping bean **is** a seed of a Mexican bush. (is, are)
2. A person actually can **see** the seed jump. (see, sees)
3. First, a moth **lays** its eggs on the bush's flowers. (lay, lays)
4. The eggs **hatch**, and caterpillars emerge. (hatch, hatches)
5. The caterpillars **burrow** into the bush's seeds. (burrow, burrows)
6. The caterpillar **eats** the inside of the seed, leaving the outer shell. (eat, eats)
7. Then, it **builds** a web inside the hollow seed. (build, builds)
8. The caterpillar **grabs** the web and wiggles its body. (grab, grabs)
9. The seed **jumps**! (jump, jumps)
10. The jumping bean **appears** active for several months. (appear, appears)

CD-104310 • © Carson-Dellosa   41

Past Tense Action Verbs and Linking Verbs (Page 42)

Remember, a past tense action verb shows action that has already happened.

Example: I *learned* about George Washington Carver yesterday.

The past tense forms of the linking verb *be* are *was* and *were*.

Example: I *was* at the party.

The past tense form of the linking verb *have* is *had*.

Example: I *had* three beans left on my plate.

The past tense form of the linking verb *become* is *became*.

Example: His research *became* important.

Write A for each sentence with a past tense action verb and L for each sentence with a past tense linking verb.

1. **L** George Washington Carver was an American scientist.
2. **L** He became famous for his agricultural research.
3. **A** Carver discovered more than 300 products from peanuts.
4. **L** He had more than 75 products from pecans.
5. **A** He developed more than 100 products from sweet potatoes.
6. **A** Carver encouraged southern farmers to try growing new crops.
7. **A** He taught farmers about keeping their crops healthy.
8. **L** Carver was head of a large research group.
9. **A** He received many awards for his contributions to science.

42   CD-104310 • © Carson-Dellosa

Forms of Be (Page 43)

The verb *be* is special because it has many forms.

When the subject of the sentence is singular, the verb *be* uses the form *am*, *is*, or *was*.

Examples: John *is* my brother.
I *am* nine years old.
Mrs. Taylor *was* my teacher.

When the subject is plural, or if the subject is you, the verb *be* uses the form *are* or *were*.

Examples: We *are* best friends.
Dan and Amy *were* on the bus.
You *are* a good student.

Remember, sometimes the forms of *be* are used as helping verbs.

Examples: We *were eating* dinner.
I *am walking* the dog.

Write the correct present tense form of the verb be to complete each sentence.

1. Mandy **is** my next-door neighbor.
2. The Taylors **are** on vacation.
3. You **are** a great friend.
4. I **am** the oldest in my family.

Write the correct past tense form of the verb be to complete the sentences.

5. Bill and Sue **were** at the movies.
6. Mom **was** at work yesterday.
7. I **was** at my aunt's house.
8. You **were** very helpful today.

CD-104310 • © Carson-Dellosa   43

Name _____

Verbs

Forms of *Be*

Be, being, and *been* are forms of the verb *be* used only after a helping verb.

Examples: Dad *will be* here in a minute.
They *were being* very polite.
I *have been* to the doctor.

Sometimes, these forms of *be* are used as helping verbs before the main verb in a sentence.

Examples: We *will be* camping at the lake.
She *was being* taken to the office.
Jeff *has been* writing a story.

Write the correct form of the verb *be* from the parentheses to complete the sentence.

1. The Gibsons have ___**been**___ to the fair.
    (been, being)

2. Rick is ___**being**___ nice to me.
    (being, be)

3. You must ___**be**___ hungry.
    (be, been)

4. The girls might ___**be**___ walking home.
    (be, being)

Write four sentences that each use the subject *I* but use different forms of the verb *be*.

5. _____**Answers will vary.**_____

6. _____

7. _____

8. _____

44   CD-104310 • © Carson-Dellosa

Name _____

Adjectives

Adjectives

An **adjective** is a word that describes a noun. An adjective tells how many or what kind. An adjective often comes in front of the noun it describes.

Examples: *Two* prairie dogs live in a burrow. (*Two* tells how many.)
Little prairie dogs are called pups. (*Little* tells what kind.)

An adjective can come after a linking verb.

Example: The prairie dog is *little.* (*Little* tells what kind.)

A sentence may have more than one adjective.

Examples: The *two* prairie dogs are *little.*
The *two little* prairie dogs are called pups.

Circle the adjective that describes each underlined noun.

1. The prairie dog lives in a (small) burrow under the ground.

2. She makes a nest of (dried) plants in the spring.

3. The prairie dog gives birth to a litter of (four) pups.

4. She is a (good) mother and stays close to her babies.

5. The pups are ready to venture outside after (six) weeks.

6. The pups have (many) friends.

CD-104310 • © Carson-Dellosa   45

Name _____

Adjectives

Adjectives

Underline the adjectives in each paragraph.

1. I like chocolate ice cream. Chocolate ice cream is good when it is hot outside. Unfortunately, chocolate ice cream makes a big, sticky mess. I solved this problem by eating my yummy chocolate ice cream outside.

2. One sunny day, I saw my neighbor's white rabbit hopping in front of my house. The rabbit seemed scared. I walked up to my neighbor's rabbit and talked to him. He hopped over to me, and I picked him up. His soft fur tickled my hands. I took the sweet rabbit home to my neighbor's house. My neighbor was happy to see his rabbit safe. The rabbit was happy to be home too.

3. Anna went to a big shoe store with her mother. Anna needed some new shoes. She saw black, shiny shoes and white shoes with ruffles. Anna especially liked the fancy red dress shoes with black and white trim. Anna decided to buy some tan shoes. Anna's mother paid the tall salesman, and Anna wore her new shoes home.

4. Shawn drove his rusty old truck home through the rain. Its tired engine rumbled, and the loud sound echoed throughout the small, quiet neighborhood. As he pulled into his wet driveway, he listened to the large drops of rain bounce on the aging metal.

46   CD-104310 • © Carson-Dellosa

Name _____

Adjectives

Adjectives That Compare

An adjective can be used to compare nouns. Add *er* to adjectives to compare two nouns. Add *est* to compare more than two nouns.

Examples: bright → brighter → brightest

If an adjective ends with *e,* drop the *e* and add *er* to compare two nouns. Drop the *e* and add *est* to compare more than two nouns.

Examples: white → whiter → whitest

If an adjective ends in a consonant that comes after a short vowel, double the final consonant and add *er* or *est.*

Examples: thin → thinner → thinnest

Write the correct forms of each adjective.

Adjectives	Adjectives That Compare Two Nouns	Adjectives That Compare More Than Two Nouns
1. long	longer	longest
2. soft	softer	softest
3. large	larger	largest
4. flat	flatter	flattest
5. sweet	sweeter	sweetest
6. wide	wider	widest
7. cool	cooler	coolest
8. smart	smarter	smartest

CD-104310 • © Carson-Dellosa   47

Proper Adjectives

A **proper adjective** is a word made from a proper noun. Proper adjectives begin with capital letters and describe nouns.

Example: The *New York* skyline is beautiful at night. (*New York* is a proper noun, but here it is used as an adjective to describe the skyline.)

Some proper adjectives are made by adding an ending to a proper noun.

Example: We ate at a *Chinese* restaurant in New York City. (*Chinese* is made from the proper noun *China*).

Write *PA* if the underlined word or words are used as proper adjectives. Write *PN* if they are used as proper nouns.

PA 1. There are many Puerto Rican neighborhoods in New York City.
PN 2. Some people have recently arrived from Puerto Rico.
PA 3. Years ago, many Irish immigrants moved to America.
PN 4. They came from Ireland in the 1800s and 1900s.
PA 5. German people immigrated to America, also.
PA 6. Some of the first English settlers were the Puritans.
PN 7. They left England for several reasons in the 1600s.
PA 8. Many people from Asian cultures came to live on the West Coast.
PA 9. There are many Korean communities in Southern California.
PA 10. American culture has been formed from many different cultures.

48   CD-104310 • © Carson-Dellosa

Articles

The words *a, an,* and *the* make up a special group of adjectives called articles. An **article** can be used before a noun or an adjective/noun combination in a sentence.

Use *a* before a singular noun that begins with a consonant.
Example: I saw *a* firefly.
Use *an* before a singular noun that begins with a vowel.
Example: Max brought *an* orange for lunch.
Use *the* before singular or plural nouns that begin with any letter.
Example: Ten apples are in *the* basket.

Circle the articles in each sentence. Underline the noun that follows each article.

1. Our dog sleeps in a doghouse.
2. The movie made us laugh.
3. I carried an umbrella in the rain.
4. Our boat had a leak.
5. Earth rotates around the sun.
6. I ate an apple and a sandwich for lunch.
7. Dad keeps the nails in an egg carton.
8. The books filled the shelf.
9. Rick saw a blue whale in the ocean.
10. An elephant likes to eat peanuts.

49

Articles

Complete each sentence with the correct article.

1. I enjoyed watching **the** game.
2. Would you like **an** egg sandwich?
3. I have **a** dog and **a** cat.
4. Did you hear **the** thunder?
5. An eagle flew over **the** house.
6. My grandmother gave me **a** new bike for my birthday.
7. The wind blew my umbrella down **the** street.
8. Mrs. Hayes said that I did **a** good job on my art project.
9. Was there **an** egg in her nest?

Write a sentence using each article.

10. a: **Answers will vary.**
11. an:
12. the:

50   CD-104310 • © Carson-Dellosa

Adverbs

An **adverb** is a word that describes a verb. Adverbs tell how, when, where, or to what extent (how much or how long) something happens.

Examples: The 100-meter dash starts tomorrow. (When?)
That runner fell down. (Where?)
The people taking tickets worked quickly. (How?)
Marathon runners run far. (How long?)

Circle the adverb in each sentence. Underline the verb that the adverb describes.

1. Janice closes the book quickly.
2. Tito frequently plays in the park.
3. Missie will watch a movie tonight.
4. Zack worked quietly on his model.
5. Leo ran on the path yesterday.
6. Pete and Susie flew to their grandma's city today.
7. Walter will miss his game tomorrow.
8. Tracy mixed the ingredients carefully.
9. Rick will eat strawberries later.
10. Ariel often stops to pick flowers.

51

Name _____ [Adjectives]

Adverbs

Circle the adverb in each sentence. Underline the verb that the adverb describes.

1. On Independence Day, we (usually) go to the parade.
2. We drive (slowly) because of the traffic.
3. The parade (often) begins with a marching band.
4. The marching band plays (loudly)
5. The huge crowd cheers (excitedly)
6. My favorite part is when the big floats pass (near) us.
7. All of the floats are decorated (beautifully)
8. We (never) see one we do not like.

Write your own sentences using the given adverbs.

9. slowly: _____ **Answers will vary.** _____

10. yesterday: _____

11. away: _____

12. there: _____

52   CD-104310 • © Carson-Dellosa

Name _____ [Adjectives]

Adverbs

Circle the adverb in each sentence. Underline the verb that the adverb describes.

1. The dogs bark (loudly) at the mail carrier.
2. I looked (everywhere) for my coat.
3. Nancy swims (faster) than I do.
4. Greg walked (slowly)
5. Valerie awoke (early)
6. Let's play (inside)

Complete each sentence with the best *how* adverb from the box. Circle the verb that the adverb describes.

quickly	beautifully	happily	better

7. The class (worked) **quickly** to finish the work before the bell.
8. I **happily** (ate) my cookie.
9. I think carrots (taste) **better** than celery.
10. We (sang) **beautifully**

Complete each sentence with the best *where* adverb from the box. Circle the verb that the adverb describes.

above	inside	there	up

11. Carlos (placed) the book **there** .
12. Donny is (waiting) **inside** for his mom.
13. The plane is (flying) **above** the clouds.
14. Ping (threw) the ball **up** in the air.

CD-104310 • © Carson-Dellosa   53

Name _____ [Adjectives]

Adverbs

Complete each sentence with the best *when* adverb from the box. Circle the verb that the adverb describes.

sometimes	now	yesterday

1. Sara (left) her shoes at the gym **yesterday** .
2. I (like) to go camping **sometimes** .
3. Since you are finished, can you (help) me **now** ?

Write one sentence using a *how* adverb, one sentence using a *where* adverb, and one sentence using a *when* adverb.

4. _____ **Answers will vary.** _____

5. _____

6. _____

Think of three different adverbs to complete this sentence:

Mark finished his homework _____.

Write your three new sentences below.

7. _____ **Answers will vary.** _____

8. _____

9. _____

54   CD-104310 • © Carson-Dellosa

Name _____ [Adjectives]

Adverbs That Compare

> Add *er* to one-syllable adverbs to compare two actions. Add *est* to one-syllable adverbs to compare more than two actions.
> Examples: Jill ran fast.
> Janell ran faster than Jill.
> Julie ran fastest of all.
> Use *more* before adverbs that end in *ly* to compare two actions. Use *most* before adverbs that end in *ly* when comparing more than two actions.
> Examples: Julie dances gracefully.
> Janell dances more gracefully than Julie.
> Jill dances most gracefully of all.

Write the correct forms of each adverb.

Adverbs	Adverbs That Compare Two Actions	Adverbs That Compare More Than Two Actions
1. quietly	more quietly	most quietly
2. strong	stronger	strongest
3. frequently	more frequently	most frequently
4. short	shorter	shortest

Complete each sentence with the correct adverb from the parentheses.

5. Mom, Tanya, and I waited **patiently** for Dad to arrive.
(patiently, more patiently)

6. We clapped **enthusiastically** for the other team.
(enthusiastically, most enthusiastically)

7. You must drive **more carefully** when the road is wet than when it is dry.
(carefully, more carefully)

CD-104310 • © Carson-Dellosa   55

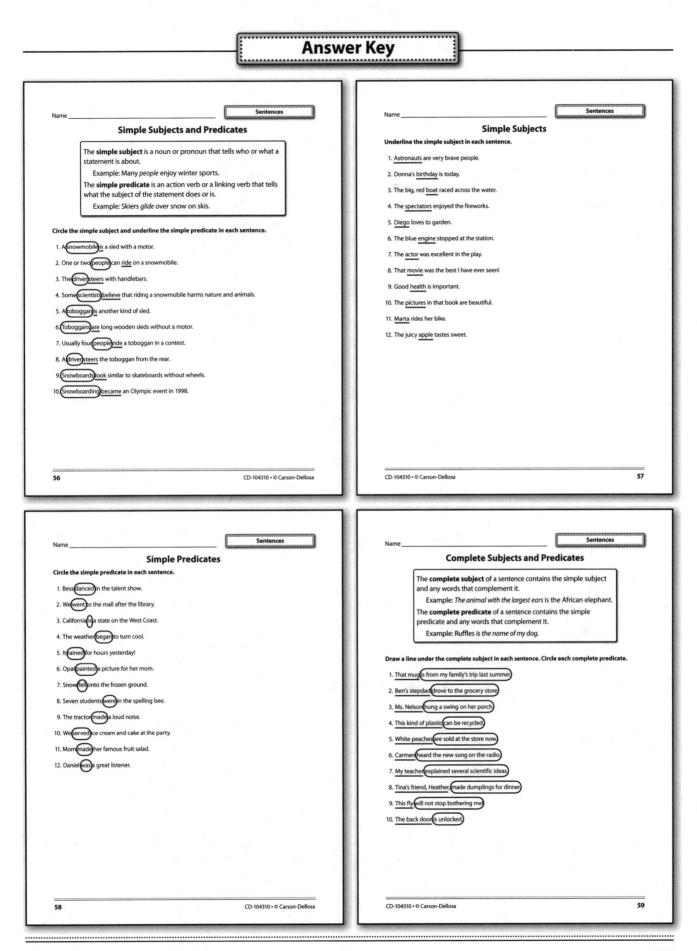

Page 56

Name _____

Sentences

Simple Subjects and Predicates

The **simple subject** is a noun or pronoun that tells who or what a statement is about.

Example: Many *people* enjoy winter sports.

The **simple predicate** is an action verb or a linking verb that tells what the subject of the statement does or is.

Example: Skiers *glide* over snow on skis.

Circle the simple subject and underline the simple predicate in each sentence.

1. A (snowmobile) is a sled with a motor.
2. One or two (people) can ride on a snowmobile.
3. The (driver) steers with handlebars.
4. Some (scientists) believe that riding a snowmobile harms nature and animals.
5. A (toboggan) is another kind of sled.
6. (Toboggans) are long wooden sleds without a motor.
7. Usually four (people) ride a toboggan in a contest.
8. A (driver) steers the toboggan from the rear.
9. (Snowboards) look similar to skateboards without wheels.
10. (Snowboarding) became an Olympic event in 1998.

56   CD-104310 • © Carson-Dellosa

Page 57

Name _____

Sentences

Simple Subjects

Underline the simple subject in each sentence.

1. Astronauts are very brave people.
2. Donna's birthday is today.
3. The big, red boat raced across the water.
4. The spectators enjoyed the fireworks.
5. Diego loves to garden.
6. The blue engine stopped at the station.
7. The actor was excellent in the play.
8. That movie was the best I have ever seen!
9. Good health is important.
10. The pictures in that book are beautiful.
11. Marta rides her bike.
12. The juicy apple tastes sweet.

CD-104310 • © Carson-Dellosa   57

Page 58

Name _____

Sentences

Simple Predicates

Circle the simple predicate in each sentence.

1. Bess (danced) in the talent show.
2. We (went) to the mall after the library.
3. California (is) a state on the West Coast.
4. The weather (began) to turn cool.
5. It (rained) for hours yesterday!
6. Opal (painted) a picture for her mom.
7. Snow (fell) onto the frozen ground.
8. Seven students (were) in the spelling bee.
9. The tractor (made) a loud noise.
10. We (served) ice cream and cake at the party.
11. Mom (made) her famous fruit salad.
12. Daniel (was) a great listener.

58   CD-104310 • © Carson-Dellosa

Page 59

Name _____

Sentences

Complete Subjects and Predicates

The **complete subject** of a sentence contains the simple subject and any words that complement it.

Example: *The animal with the largest ears* is the African elephant.

The **complete predicate** of a sentence contains the simple predicate and any words that complement it.

Example: Ruffles *is the name of my dog.*

Draw a line under the complete subject in each sentence. Circle each complete predicate.

1. That mug (is from my family's trip last summer.)
2. Ben's stepdad (drove to the grocery store.)
3. Ms. Nelson (hung a swing on her porch.)
4. This kind of plastic (can be recycled.)
5. White peaches (are sold at the store now.)
6. Carmen (heard the new song on the radio.)
7. My teacher (explained several scientific ideas.)
8. Tina's friend, Heather, (made dumplings for dinner.)
9. This fly (will not stop bothering me!)
10. The back door (is unlocked.)

CD-104310 • © Carson-Dellosa   59

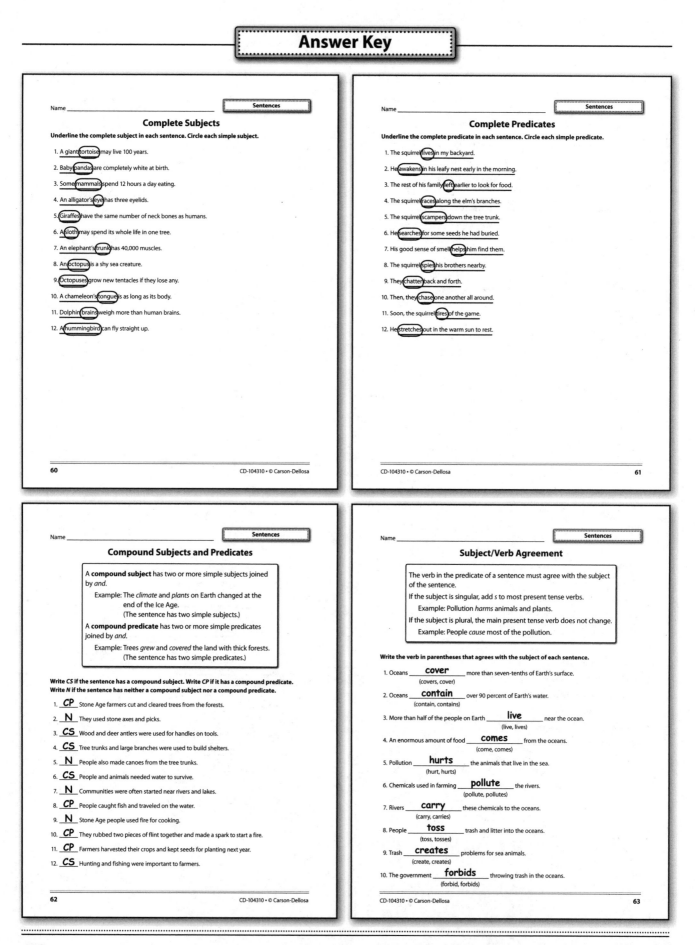

Name _____   Sentences

Complete Subjects

Underline the complete subject in each sentence. Circle each simple subject.

1. A giant (tortoise) may live 100 years.

2. Baby (pandas) are completely white at birth.

3. Some (mammals) spend 12 hours a day eating.

4. An alligator's (eye) has three eyelids.

5. (Giraffes) have the same number of neck bones as humans.

6. A (sloth) may spend its whole life in one tree.

7. An elephant's (trunk) has 40,000 muscles.

8. An (octopus) is a shy sea creature.

9. (Octopuses) grow new tentacles if they lose any.

10. A chameleon's (tongue) is as long as its body.

11. Dolphin (brains) weigh more than human brains.

12. A (hummingbird) can fly straight up.

60   CD-104310 • © Carson-Dellosa

Name _____   Sentences

Complete Predicates

Underline the complete predicate in each sentence. Circle each simple predicate.

1. The squirrel (lives) in my backyard.

2. He (awakens) in his leafy nest early in the morning.

3. The rest of his family (left) earlier to look for food.

4. The squirrel (races) along the elm's branches.

5. The squirrel (scampers) down the tree trunk.

6. He (searches) for some seeds he had buried.

7. His good sense of smell (helps) him find them.

8. The squirrel (spies) his brothers nearby.

9. They (chatter) back and forth.

10. Then, they (chase) one another all around.

11. Soon, the squirrel (tires) of the game.

12. He (stretches) out in the warm sun to rest.

CD-104310 • © Carson-Dellosa   61

Name _____   Sentences

Compound Subjects and Predicates

> A **compound subject** has two or more simple subjects joined by *and*.
>> Example: The *climate* and *plants* on Earth changed at the end of the Ice Age.
>> (The sentence has two simple subjects.)
>
> A **compound predicate** has two or more simple predicates joined by *and*.
>> Example: Trees *grew* and *covered* the land with thick forests.
>> (The sentence has two simple predicates.)

Write CS if the sentence has a compound subject. Write CP if it has a compound predicate. Write N if the sentence has neither a compound subject nor a compound predicate.

1. __CP__ Stone Age farmers cut and cleared trees from the forests.

2. __N__ They used stone axes and picks.

3. __CS__ Wood and deer antlers were used for handles on tools.

4. __CS__ Tree trunks and large branches were used to build shelters.

5. __N__ People also made canoes from the tree trunks.

6. __CS__ People and animals needed water to survive.

7. __N__ Communities were often started near rivers and lakes.

8. __CP__ People caught fish and traveled on the water.

9. __N__ Stone Age people used fire for cooking.

10. __CP__ They rubbed two pieces of flint together and made a spark to start a fire.

11. __CP__ Farmers harvested their crops and kept seeds for planting next year.

12. __CS__ Hunting and fishing were important to farmers.

62   CD-104310 • © Carson-Dellosa

Name _____   Sentences

Subject/Verb Agreement

> The verb in the predicate of a sentence must agree with the subject of the sentence.
> If the subject is singular, add *s* to most present tense verbs.
>> Example: Pollution *harms* animals and plants.
> If the subject is plural, the main present tense verb does not change.
>> Example: People *cause* most of the pollution.

Write the verb in parentheses that agrees with the subject of each sentence.

1. Oceans __cover__ more than seven-tenths of Earth's surface.
(covers, cover)

2. Oceans __contain__ over 90 percent of Earth's water.
(contain, contains)

3. More than half of the people on Earth __live__ near the ocean.
(live, lives)

4. An enormous amount of food __comes__ from the oceans.
(come, comes)

5. Pollution __hurts__ the animals that live in the sea.
(hurt, hurts)

6. Chemicals used in farming __pollute__ the rivers.
(pollute, pollutes)

7. Rivers __carry__ these chemicals to the oceans.
(carry, carries)

8. People __toss__ trash and litter into the oceans.
(toss, tosses)

9. Trash __creates__ problems for sea animals.
(create, creates)

10. The government __forbids__ throwing trash in the oceans.
(forbid, forbids)

CD-104310 • © Carson-Dellosa   63

Subject/Verb Agreement

> A compound subject is like a plural subject. It has two or more simple subjects joined by *and*. The main present tense verb does not change.
> Example: The saguaro and other cactuses *produce* flowers.
> Add *s* to most present tense verbs when the subject pronoun is *she, he,* or *it*.
> Example: She *grows* cactuses.
> The main verb does not change when the subject pronoun is *I, we, you,* or *they*.
> Example: They *grow* flowers.

Write the verb that agrees with the subject of each sentence.

1. Most cacti **grow** in hot, dry places.
   (grow, grows)

2. They **vary** in size and shape.
   (vary, varies)

3. The height of some cacti **reaches** 60 feet.
   (reach, reaches)

4. Some varieties of cacti **look** like porcupines.
   (look, looks)

5. Thick, fleshy stems and long roots **help** cacti survive.
   (help, helps)

6. The stem **holds** water.
   (hold, holds)

7. The cactus's waxy skin **keeps** water near the cactus.
   (keep, keeps)

8. Its long roots **gather** water after a rain.
   (gather, gathers)

Declarative and Interrogative Sentences

> A **declarative sentence** tells something and ends with a period. It makes a statement.
> Example: Animals live in each country.
> An **interrogative sentence** asks a question and ends with a question mark.
> Example: What kind of animals live in your country?

Add the correct punctuation mark at the end of each sentence. Answer the question with a declarative sentence using the information given.

1. Where do kangaroos live **?**
   Kangaroos live where koalas live **.**
   Koalas live in Australia **.**
   Kangaroos live in Australia.

2. Most wild penguins live south of the equator **.**
   Do wild penguins live in Antarctica **?**
   Antarctica is south of the equator **.**
   Wild penguins live in Antarctica.

3. Monarch butterflies migrate to Michigan in the spring **.**
   These butterflies migrate to Mexico in the fall **.**
   Are monarch butterflies in Michigan in the winter **?**
   Monarch butterflies are not in Michigan in the winter.

4. Do orangutans live in the Brazilian rain forest **?**
   The Brazilian rain forest is in South America **.**
   Orangutans live in a small part of Southeast Asia **.**
   Orangutans do not live in the Brazilian rain forest.

Exclamatory Sentences

> An **exclamatory sentence** shows strong feeling and ends with an exclamation mark.
> Example: This is the best birthday ever!

Rewrite each exclamatory sentence. Add capital letters where they belong and exclamation marks at the end of each exclamatory sentence.

1. this dessert is delicious
   This dessert is delicious!

2. that comet is beautiful
   That comet is beautiful!

3. we're going to florida
   We're going to Florida!

4. ouch, get off my foot
   Ouch, get off my foot!

5. you startled me
   You startled me!

6. the fireworks are incredible
   The fireworks are incredible!

7. listen to that thunder
   Listen to that thunder!

8. wow, your picture looks great
   Wow, your picture looks great!

Declarative, Interrogative, and Exclamatory Sentences

For each sentence, write *D* for declarative, *I* for interrogative, or *E* for exclamatory. Add the correct punctuation mark at the end of each sentence. Circle the letters that should be capitalized.

1. **D** Our class is going to the amusement park **.**
2. **D** The bus will leave early **.**
3. **I** Did you set your alarm clock **?**
4. **D** Abby and I stood in line together **.**
5. **E** Yikes, the food here is expensive **!**
6. **I** Did you bring lunch **?**
7. **D** I'm glad I did **.**
8. **D** We put our lunches on the tables **.**
9. **E** Let's go to the rides **!**
10. **D** Mona, Julie, Max, and I got in line for a roller coaster **.**
11. **D** We put on our seat belts and harnesses **.**
12. **E** I'm scared **!**

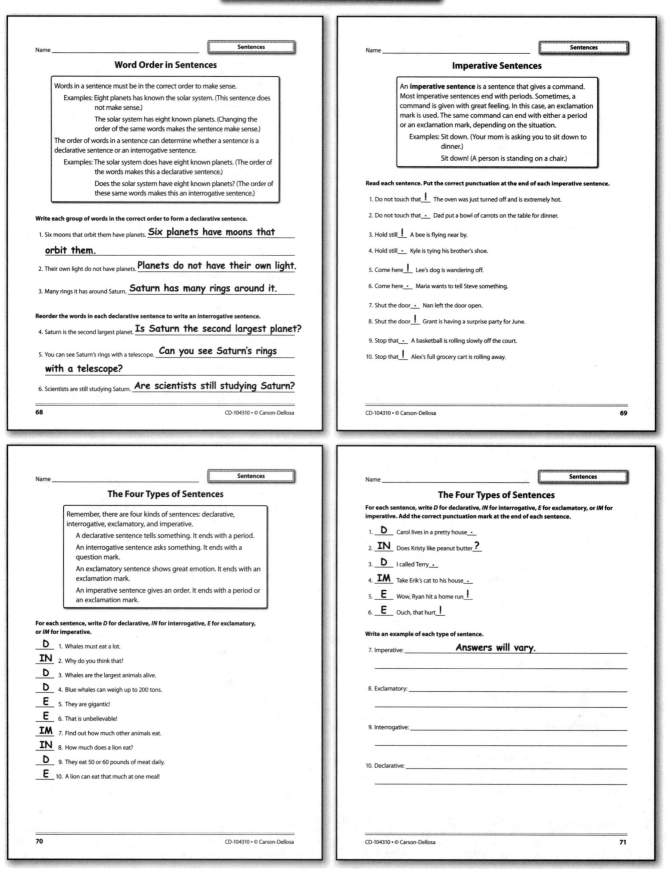

Name _____   Sentences

Word Order in Sentences

Words in a sentence must be in the correct order to make sense.
Examples: Eight planets has known the solar system. (This sentence does not make sense.)
The solar system has eight known planets. (Changing the order of the same words makes the sentence make sense.)
The order of words in a sentence can determine whether a sentence is a declarative sentence or an interrogative sentence.
Examples: The solar system does have eight known planets. (The order of the words makes this a declarative sentence.)
Does the solar system have eight known planets? (The order of these same words makes this an interrogative sentence.)

Write each group of words in the correct order to form a declarative sentence.

1. Six moons that orbit them have planets. Six planets have moons that orbit them.

2. Their own light do not have planets. Planets do not have their own light.

3. Many rings it has around Saturn. Saturn has many rings around it.

Reorder the words in each declarative sentence to write an interrogative sentence.

4. Saturn is the second largest planet. Is Saturn the second largest planet?

5. You can see Saturn's rings with a telescope. Can you see Saturn's rings with a telescope?

6. Scientists are still studying Saturn. Are scientists still studying Saturn?

68   CD-104310 • © Carson-Dellosa

Name _____   Sentences

Imperative Sentences

An **imperative sentence** is a sentence that gives a command. Most imperative sentences end with periods. Sometimes, a command is given with great feeling. In this case, an exclamation mark is used. The same command can end with either a period or an exclamation mark, depending on the situation.
Examples: Sit down. (Your mom is asking you to sit down to dinner.)
Sit down! (A person is standing on a chair.)

Read each sentence. Put the correct punctuation at the end of each imperative sentence.

1. Do not touch that **!** The oven was just turned off and is extremely hot.

2. Do not touch that **.** Dad put a bowl of carrots on the table for dinner.

3. Hold still **!** A bee is flying near by.

4. Hold still **.** Kyle is tying his brother's shoe.

5. Come here **!** Lee's dog is wandering off.

6. Come here **.** Maria wants to tell Steve something.

7. Shut the door **.** Nan left the door open.

8. Shut the door **!** Grant is having a surprise party for June.

9. Stop that **.** A basketball is rolling slowly off the court.

10. Stop that **!** Alex's full grocery cart is rolling away.

CD-104310 • © Carson-Dellosa   69

Name _____   Sentences

The Four Types of Sentences

Remember, there are four kinds of sentences: declarative, interrogative, exclamatory, and imperative.
A declarative sentence tells something. It ends with a period.
An interrogative sentence asks something. It ends with a question mark.
An exclamatory sentence shows great emotion. It ends with an exclamation mark.
An imperative sentence gives an order. It ends with a period or an exclamation mark.

For each sentence, write _D_ for declarative, _IN_ for interrogative, _E_ for exclamatory, or _IM_ for imperative.

D 1. Whales must eat a lot.

IN 2. Why do you think that?

D 3. Whales are the largest animals alive.

D 4. Blue whales can weigh up to 200 tons.

E 5. They are gigantic!

E 6. That is unbelievable!

IM 7. Find out how much other animals eat.

IN 8. How much does a lion eat?

D 9. They eat 50 or 60 pounds of meat daily.

E 10. A lion can eat that much at one meal!

70   CD-104310 • © Carson-Dellosa

Name _____   Sentences

The Four Types of Sentences

For each sentence, write _D_ for declarative, _IN_ for interrogative, _E_ for exclamatory, or _IM_ for imperative. Add the correct punctuation mark at the end of each sentence.

1. **D** Carol lives in a pretty house **.**

2. **IN** Does Kristy like peanut butter **?**

3. **D** I called Terry **.**

4. **IM** Take Erik's cat to his house **.**

5. **E** Wow, Ryan hit a home run **!**

6. **E** Ouch, that hurt **!**

Write an example of each type of sentence.

7. Imperative: _____ Answers will vary. _____

8. Exclamatory: _____

9. Interrogative: _____

10. Declarative: _____

CD-104310 • © Carson-Dellosa   71

Name _____ [Sentences]

Commas

Commas can be used to separate words in a series or list.
Example: Grapefruit, oranges, tangerines, and lemons are citrus fruits.

Rewrite each sentence below, using commas where they are needed.

1. My favorite sports are soccer basketball and tennis.
   My favorite sports are soccer, basketball, and tennis.

2. Remember to grab your lunch box book bag and raincoat for school.
   Remember to grab your lunch box, book bag, and raincoat for school.

3. I want cheese garlic and green pepper on my pizza.
   I want cheese, garlic, and green pepper on my pizza.

4. My duties are to dust feed the cat and take out the trash.
   My chores are to dust, feed the cat, and take out the trash.

5. Please stop by the store for cereal milk and orange juice.
   Please stop by the store for cereal, milk, and orange juice.

72   CD-104310 • © Carson-Dellosa

Name _____ [Sentences]

Commas

A comma or commas can be used to set apart the name of the person being spoken to directly from the rest of the sentence.
Examples: Where can I learn more about falcons, Alex?
You know, Kim, that falcons are birds of prey.

Commas can be used to separate an appositive that immediately follows a noun from the rest of the sentence. An appositive is a word or phrase that explains or identifies a noun.
Examples: Falcons, birds of prey, live on rocky cliffs. (The phrase *birds of prey* identifies and explains the noun *falcons*.)
Some birds of prey, such as falcons, live on rocky cliffs. (The phrase *such as falcons* identifies the phrase *Some birds of prey*.)

A comma can be used to separate the two parts of a compound sentence.
Example: There are about 40 species of falcons, and half of the species are found in Africa.

The proofreading mark (∧) is used to show where a word or punctuation mark needs to be inserted or added. Use the proofreading mark (∧) to show where each comma is needed in the sentences.

1. Kim∧ let's look at this book about falcons.

2. Birds of prey∧ such as hawks∧ have hooked beaks and feet with claws.

3. Falcons are powerful fliers∧ and they can swoop from great heights.

4. The American kestrel∧ the smallest North American falcon∧ is only 8 inches long.

5. A bird of prey∧ the American kestrel∧ eats insects∧ mice∧ lizards∧ and other birds.

CD-104310 • © Carson-Dellosa   73

Name _____ [Sentences]

Fragments

A **fragment** is an incomplete sentence that does not express a complete thought.
Examples: Anna and Beth went swimming. (sentence)
Anna and Beth. (missing a predicate that tells what happened)
Went swimming. (missing a subject that tells who)

Write S for each sentence and F for each fragment.

1. **F** Rang loudly and woke all of us!
2. **F** Down the dark tunnel and into a large cave.
3. **F** Pete and his cousin, Elmo.
4. **S** We will play a game after dinner.
5. **S** You may come along with us.
6. **S** The darts hit the board.
7. **F** Around the corner and over the bridge.
8. **S** That is my house.
9. **S** Frank ate the beans.
10. **F** A sandwich and some carrot sticks.
11. **S** She is a shy girl.
12. **F** The states of Texas, Michigan, and New York.

74   CD-104310 • © Carson-Dellosa

Name _____ [Sentences]

Run-On Sentences

When two independent clauses are written together, they create a run-on sentence. To avoid a run-on sentence, decide where the first sentence ends and the second begins. A run-on sentence can be corrected by separating it into two or more sentences.
Example: Casey is helpful he sets the table every night. (run-on sentence)
Casey is helpful. He sets the table every night. (corrected)

Separate each run-on sentence into two sentences. Put a punctuation mark at the end of the first sentence. Cross out the lowercase letter and write a capital letter above the first letter in the next word to begin the second sentence.

1. Raven has a new backpack it is green with many zippers.
   Raven has a new backpack. It is green with many zippers.
2. Ray needs a paper clip he needs it to hold his papers.
   Ray needs a paper clip. He needs it to hold his papers.
3. Katie borrowed my pencil she plans to draw a map.
   Katie borrowed my pencil. She plans to draw a map.
4. It is so cold the driveway is covered with ice.
   It is so cold! The driveway is covered with ice.
5. Jane is outside she is on the swings.
   Jane is outside. She is on the swings.
6. Zack is helping Dad Elroy is helping Dad, too.
   Zack is helping Dad. Elroy is helping Dad, too.
7. Keesha read that book she recommended it to the class.
   Keesha read that book. She recommended it to the class.
8. Tori saw a baby squirrel it was at the bottom of that tree.
   Tori saw a baby squirrel. It was lying at the bottom of that tree.
9. Zeke loves cinnamon rolls the ones with the nuts are his favorite.
   Zeke loves cinnamon rolls. The ones with the nuts are his favorite.
10. Turn off the light it has been on too long.
    Turn off the light. It has been on too long.

CD-104310 • © Carson-Dellosa   75

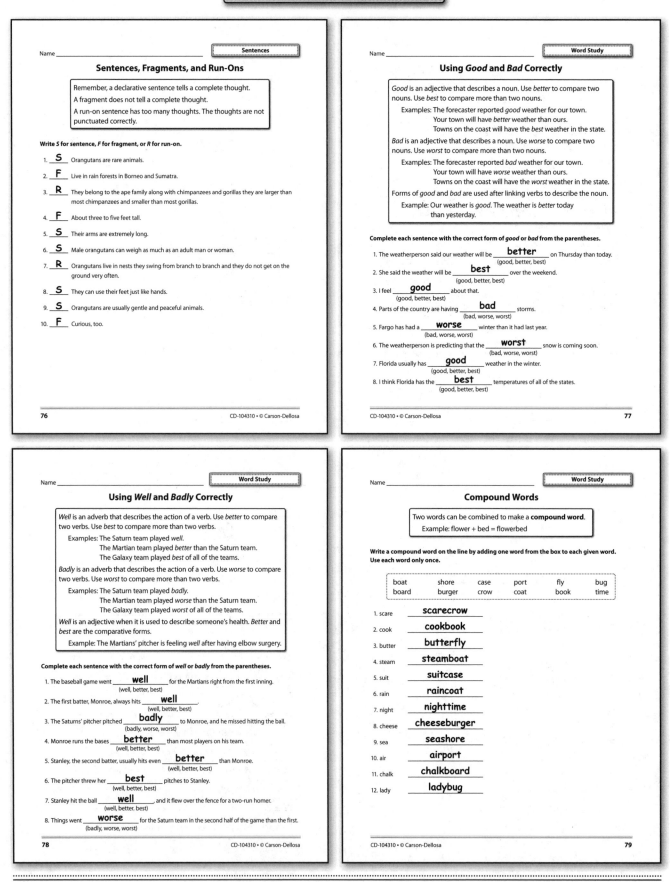

Name _____

Sentences

Sentences, Fragments, and Run-Ons

Remember, a declarative sentence tells a complete thought.
A fragment does not tell a complete thought.
A run-on sentence has too many thoughts. The thoughts are not punctuated correctly.

Write *S* for sentence, *F* for fragment, or *R* for run-on.

1. **S** Orangutans are rare animals.

2. **F** Live in rain forests in Borneo and Sumatra.

3. **R** They belong to the ape family along with chimpanzees and gorillas they are larger than most chimpanzees and smaller than most gorillas.

4. **F** About three to five feet tall.

5. **S** Their arms are extremely long.

6. **S** Male orangutans can weigh as much as an adult man or woman.

7. **R** Orangutans live in nests they swing from branch to branch and they do not get on the ground very often.

8. **S** They can use their feet just like hands.

9. **S** Orangutans are usually gentle and peaceful animals.

10. **F** Curious, too.

76
CD-104310 • © Carson-Dellosa

Name _____

Word Study

Using *Good* and *Bad* Correctly

Good is an adjective that describes a noun. Use *better* to compare two nouns. Use *best* to compare more than two nouns.

Examples: The forecaster reported *good* weather for our town.
Your town will have *better* weather than ours.
Towns on the coast will have the *best* weather in the state.

Bad is an adjective that describes a noun. Use *worse* to compare two nouns. Use *worst* to compare more than two nouns.

Examples: The forecaster reported *bad* weather for our town.
Your town will have *worse* weather than ours.
Towns on the coast will have the *worst* weather in the state.

Forms of *good* and *bad* are used after linking verbs to describe the noun.

Example: Our weather is *good*. The weather is *better* today than yesterday.

Complete each sentence with the correct form of *good* or *bad* from the parentheses.

1. The weatherperson said our weather will be **better** on Thursday than today.
(good, better, best)

2. She said the weather will be **best** over the weekend.
(good, better, best)

3. I feel **good** about that.
(good, better, best)

4. Parts of the country are having **bad** storms.
(bad, worse, worst)

5. Fargo has had a **worse** winter than it had last year.
(bad, worse, worst)

6. The weatherperson is predicting that the **worst** snow is coming soon.
(bad, worse, worst)

7. Florida usually has **good** weather in the winter.
(good, better, best)

8. I think Florida has the **best** temperatures of all of the states.
(good, better, best)

CD-104310 • © Carson-Dellosa
77

Name _____

Word Study

Using *Well* and *Badly* Correctly

Well is an adverb that describes the action of a verb. Use *better* to compare two verbs. Use *best* to compare more than two verbs.

Examples: The Saturn team played *well*.
The Martian team played *better* than the Saturn team.
The Galaxy team played *best* of all of the teams.

Badly is an adverb that describes the action of a verb. Use *worse* to compare two verbs. Use *worst* to compare more than two verbs.

Examples: The Saturn team played *badly*.
The Martian team played *worse* than the Saturn team.
The Galaxy team played *worst* of all of the teams.

Well is an adjective when it is used to describe someone's health. *Better* and *best* are the comparative forms.

Example: The Martians' pitcher is feeling *well* after having elbow surgery.

Complete each sentence with the correct form of *well* or *badly* from the parentheses.

1. The baseball game went **well** for the Martians right from the first inning.
(well, better, best)

2. The first batter, Monroe, always hits **well**.
(well, better, best)

3. The Saturns' pitcher pitched **badly** to Monroe, and he missed hitting the ball.
(badly, worse, worst)

4. Monroe runs the bases **better** than most players on his team.
(well, better, best)

5. Stanley, the second batter, usually hits even **better** than Monroe.
(well, better, best)

6. The pitcher threw her **best** pitches to Stanley.
(well, better, best)

7. Stanley hit the ball **well**, and it flew over the fence for a two-run homer.
(well, better, best)

8. Things went **worse** for the Saturn team in the second half of the game than the first.
(badly, worse, worst)

78
CD-104310 • © Carson-Dellosa

Name _____

Word Study

Compound Words

Two words can be combined to make a **compound word**.
Example: flower + bed = flowerbed

Write a compound word on the line by adding one word from the box to each given word. Use each word only once.

| boat | shore | case | port | fly | bug |
| board | burger | crow | coat | book | time |

1. scare   **scarecrow**

2. cook   **cookbook**

3. butter   **butterfly**

4. steam   **steamboat**

5. suit   **suitcase**

6. rain   **raincoat**

7. night   **nighttime**

8. cheese   **cheeseburger**

9. sea   **seashore**

10. air   **airport**

11. chalk   **chalkboard**

12. lady   **ladybug**

CD-104310 • © Carson-Dellosa
79

Answer Key

Contractions

A **contraction** is made by joining two words to make one new word. In a contraction, one or more letters from the words that it is made of are left out. An apostrophe (') is used in place of the left-out letter or letters. Some contractions are made from a verb and the word *not*.

Examples: do not → don't
cannot → can't
will not → won't

Write each contraction as a pair of words.

1. wouldn't — would not
2. haven't — have not
3. aren't — are not
4. doesn't — does not

Write each pair of words as a contraction.

5. had not — hadn't
6. did not — didn't
7. should not — shouldn't
8. has not — hasn't

80 CD-104310 • © Carson-Dellosa

Contractions

Some contractions are made by joining a pronoun and a linking verb.
Example: I am → I'm (An apostrophe takes the place of the *a* in *am*.)
Some contractions are made by joining a pronoun with *will* or *would*.
Examples: I will → I'll (An apostrophe takes the place of the *wi* in *will*.)
I would → I'd (An apostrophe takes the place of the *woul* in *would*.)

Write each contraction as a pair of words.

1. she'll — she will
2. he'd — he would
3. you've — you have
4. she's — she is

Write each pair of words as a contraction.

5. you are — you're
6. she would — she'd
7. they have — they've
8. he will — he'll

CD-104310 • © Carson-Dellosa 81

Contractions

Write each word or pair of words as a contraction.

1. she will — she'll
2. you are — you're
3. he would — he'd
4. there is — there's
5. I am — I'm
6. cannot — can't
7. they are — they're
8. should not — shouldn't
9. what is — what's
10. they will — they'll
11. we would — we'd
12. we are — we're

82 CD-104310 • © Carson-Dellosa

Contractions

Complete the story by writing the correct contraction from the box in each blank. Use each contraction only once.

can't	can't	She'll	they're
we'll	it'll	won't	we've
it's	I've	we're	won't

I am happy because **it's** my mother's birthday today. I am really excited because my father and **I've** made special plans. For weeks, **we've** been planning her birthday. There is a terrific restaurant downtown. I **can't** remember its name, but **we're** taking Mom there for dinner. My grandparents **won't** be able to meet us at the restaurant, but **they're** coming to our house later. That is when **we'll** be having cake and ice cream. Mom **won't** be expecting to see my grandparents because she thinks they are still on vacation. There will be lots of presents for my mom to open. **She'll** be so surprised! I **can't** wait until tonight. I know **it'll** be the best birthday my mom ever had!

CD-104310 • © Carson-Dellosa 83

CD-104310 • © Carson-Dellosa **123**

Answer Key

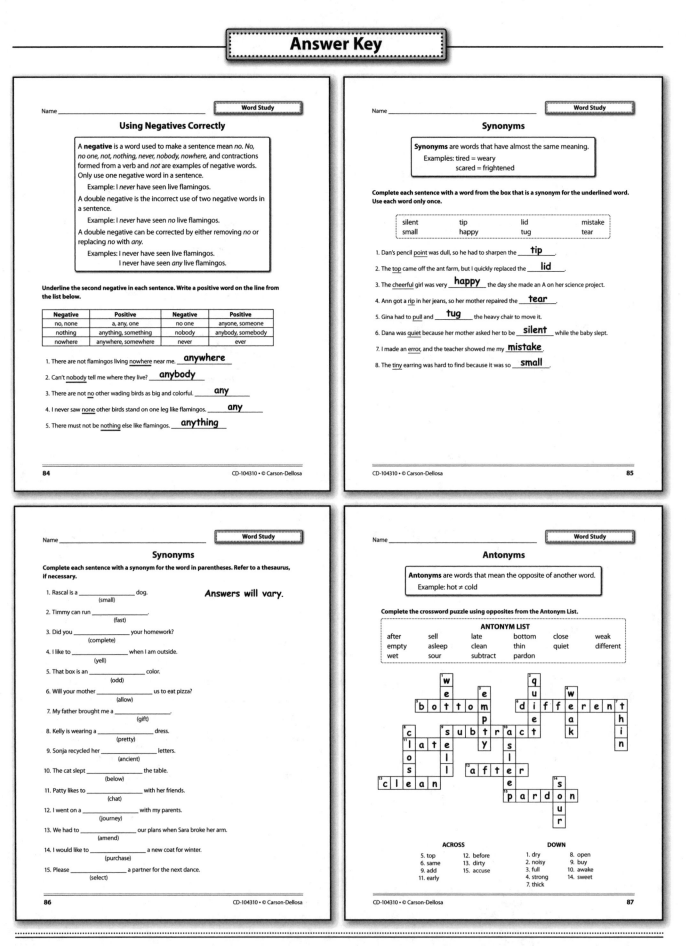

Name _____

Antonyms

Write an antonym for each word. Refer to a thesaurus, if necessary.

Answers will vary.

1. ill _____
2. soft _____
3. smile _____
4. first _____
5. begin _____
6. arrive _____
7. light _____
8. lost _____
9. old _____
10. over _____
11. give _____
12. forward _____
13. stop _____
14. always _____

88   CD-104310 • © Carson-Dellosa

Name _____

Homophones

Homophones are words that are pronounced the same, but are spelled differently and have different meanings. Homophones can be confusing when you hear them.

Example: The *prince prints* books. (*Prince* and *prints* sound alike, but *prince* is a male in a royal family and *prints* means "to publish" in this sentence.)

Complete each sentence with the correct homophone from the parentheses. Refer to a dictionary, if necessary.

1. The U.S. Coast Guard may use a small **or** large boat to help people in trouble in the water. (oar, or)

2. They **know** how to stay safe when helping other people. (know, no)

3. Rescuers **use** small boats close to shore. (ewes, use)

4. Large boats have powerful radios and equipment **for** navigation. (for, four)

5. They have first aid kits and survival gear on **board** their boats. (board, bored)

6. The Coast Guard can **tow** a ship to shore. (toe, tow)

7. Rescues at **sea** are often difficult. (sea, see)

8. For example, last year a **lone** sailor was in trouble. (loan, lone)

9. The Coast Guard raced to the **scene** in a helicopter. (scene, seen)

10. Choose five homophones you did not use as correct answers in the sentences above. On another sheet of paper, write a sentence for each one. Refer to a dictionary, if necessary.

Answers will vary.

CD-104310 • © Carson-Dellosa   89

Name _____

Prefixes

A **prefix** is a group of letters added to the beginning of a word. A prefix adds meaning or changes the word's meaning. The word to which the prefix is added is called the root word or base word. When adding a prefix, the spelling of the root word is not changed.

Some common prefixes and their meanings are:
re: again   pre: before   un, dis, mis: not or against   bi: two   uni: one

Draw a line from each word to its correct meaning.

1. unhappy — not happy
2. bicycle — cycle with two wheels
3. review — view again
4. uncover — not cover
5. unlimited — not limited
6. prewritten — written before
7. bimonthly — every two months
8. unknown — not known
9. unicycle — cycle with one wheel

Underline the word with a prefix in each sentence. Write the meaning of the word on the line.

10. Anabelle's umbrella stayed <u>unopened</u> until it began to rain. **not opened**

11. Cicily bought <u>prewashed</u> jeans. **washed before**

12. Sam is going for his <u>biweekly</u> allergy shot. **every two weeks**

90   CD-104310 • © Carson-Dellosa

Name _____

Prefixes

Use the Prefix List and Root Word List to create as many words as you can. Use another sheet of paper if necessary.

PREFIX LIST				
dis	in	pre	re	un

ROOT WORD LIST					
able	miss	charge	heat	fill	wind
form	capable	qualify	cover	pay	close
related	view				

Answers will vary.

1. _____   12. _____
2. _____   13. _____
3. _____   14. _____
4. _____   15. _____
5. _____   16. _____
6. _____   17. _____
7. _____   18. _____
8. _____   19. _____
9. _____   20. _____
10. _____   21. _____
11. _____   22. _____

CD-104310 • © Carson-Dellosa   91

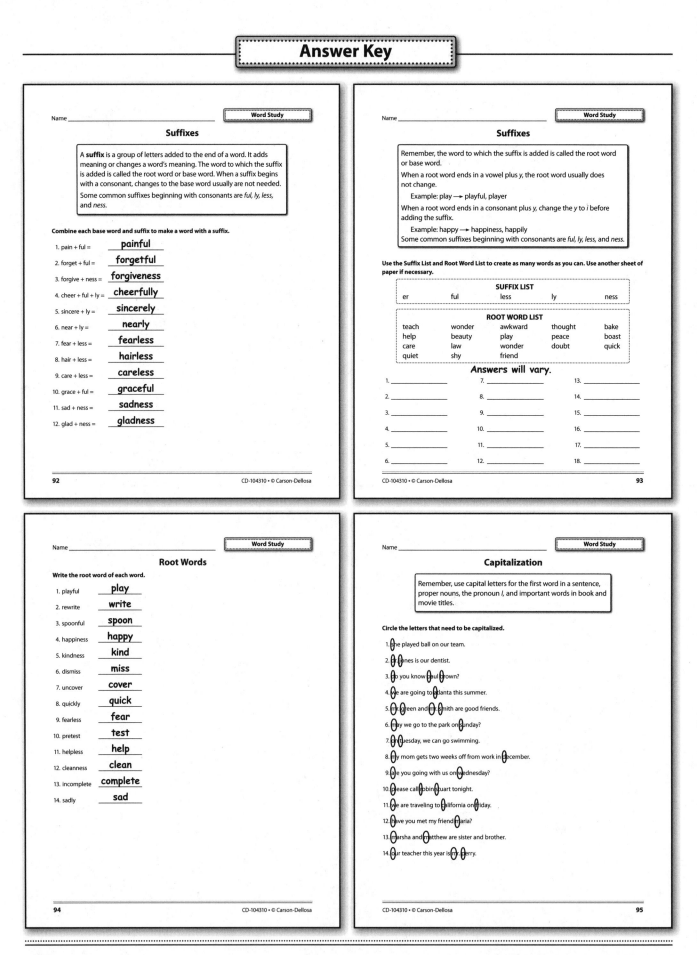

Name _____

Suffixes

A **suffix** is a group of letters added to the end of a word. It adds meaning or changes a word's meaning. The word to which the suffix is added is called the root word or base word. When a suffix begins with a consonant, changes to the base word usually are not needed. Some common suffixes beginning with consonants are *ful, ly, less,* and *ness*.

Combine each base word and suffix to make a word with a suffix.

1. pain + ful = **painful**
2. forget + ful = **forgetful**
3. forgive + ness = **forgiveness**
4. cheer + ful + ly = **cheerfully**
5. sincere + ly = **sincerely**
6. near + ly = **nearly**
7. fear + less = **fearless**
8. hair + less = **hairless**
9. care + less = **careless**
10. grace + ful = **graceful**
11. sad + ness = **sadness**
12. glad + ness = **gladness**

92   CD-104310 • © Carson-Dellosa

Name _____

Suffixes

Remember, the word to which the suffix is added is called the root word or base word.

When a root word ends in a vowel plus *y*, the root word usually does not change.

    Example: play → playful, player

When a root word ends in a consonant plus *y*, change the *y* to *i* before adding the suffix.

    Example: happy → happiness, happily

Some common suffixes beginning with consonants are *ful, ly, less,* and *ness*.

Use the Suffix List and Root Word List to create as many words as you can. Use another sheet of paper if necessary.

SUFFIX LIST				
er	ful	less	ly	ness

ROOT WORD LIST				
teach	wonder	awkward	thought	bake
help	beauty	play	peace	boast
care	law	wonder	doubt	quick
quiet	shy	friend		

Answers will vary.

1. _____   7. _____   13. _____
2. _____   8. _____   14. _____
3. _____   9. _____   15. _____
4. _____   10. _____   16. _____
5. _____   11. _____   17. _____
6. _____   12. _____   18. _____

CD-104310 • © Carson-Dellosa   93

Name _____

Root Words

Write the root word of each word.

1. playful   **play**
2. rewrite   **write**
3. spoonful   **spoon**
4. happiness   **happy**
5. kindness   **kind**
6. dismiss   **miss**
7. uncover   **cover**
8. quickly   **quick**
9. fearless   **fear**
10. pretest   **test**
11. helpless   **help**
12. cleanness   **clean**
13. incomplete **complete**
14. sadly   **sad**

94   CD-104310 • © Carson-Dellosa

Name _____

Capitalization

Remember, use capital letters for the first word in a sentence, proper nouns, the pronoun *I*, and important words in book and movie titles.

Circle the letters that need to be capitalized.

1. (S)he played ball on our team.
2. (D)r. (J)ones is our dentist.
3. (D)o you know (P)aul (B)rown?
4. (W)e are going to (A)tlanta this summer.
5. (M)r. (G)reen and (M)r. (S)mith are good friends.
6. (M)ay we go to the park on (S)unday?
7. (O)n (T)uesday, we can go swimming.
8. (M)y mom gets two weeks off from work in (D)ecember.
9. (A)re you going with us on (W)ednesday?
10. (P)lease call (R)obin (S)tuart tonight.
11. (W)e are traveling to (C)alifornia on (F)riday.
12. (H)ave you met my friend (M)aria?
13. (M)arsha and (M)atthew are sister and brother.
14. (O)ur teacher this year is (M)r. (P)erry.

CD-104310 • © Carson-Dellosa   95

Name _____

Capitalization

Each sentence has one or more capitalization mistakes. Write each sentence correctly on the line below.

1. laura ingalls wilder wrote the book little house on the prairie.

   Laura Ingalls Wilder wrote the book Little House on the Prairie.

2. my friend shelly moved to pennsylvania.

   My friend Shelly moved to Pennsylvania.

3. i will go visit grandma hazel next summer.

   I will go visit Grandma Hazel next summer.

4. last saturday, we went to see the movie the lost treasure.

   Last Saturday, we went to see the movie The Lost Treasure.

5. our neighbor, mr. johnson, lets us fish in his pond.

   Our neighbor, Mr. Johnson, lets us fish in his pond.

6. I like to shop at saunders shoes at the mall.

   I like to shop at Saunders Shoes at the mall.

7. we named our new kitten muffin.

   We named our new kitten Muffin.

8. we always go to the fair in september.

   We always go to the fair in September.

96   CD-104310 • © Carson-Dellosa

Name _____

Capitalization

> Capitalize the first letter of a person's first and last name.
>
> Examples: I spoke with *Tommy* today.
> She gave *Nancy Connor* a gift.
>
> Capitalize a personal title when it is in front of a person's name.
>
> Example: *President* Patricia Garcia and *Mr.* Hank Parker are coming to dinner.

Cross out each word in the paragraph that needs a capital letter. Write the word with the correct capital letter in the space above the crossed-out word.

Pocahontas
pocahontas was a Native American who lived in Virginia during the time of the first English settlement.

Pocahontas   Captain John Smith
According to legend, pocahontas saved the life of captain john smith. Later, she moved into

Rebecca   Mr. John Rolfe
Jamestown and took the name rebecca. She married mr. john rolfe, and they traveled to England to

King James Pocahontas   Thomas
meet king james. pocahontas died in England and was buried there. She had one son, thomas.

CD-104310 • © Carson-Dellosa   97

Name _____

Capitalization

> Capitalize the names of geographical places, such as cities, states, countries, and continents.
>
> Example: *California* is in the *United States*, on the continent of *North America*.
>
> Capitalize the names of important man-made places.
>
> Example: They went to see the *Statue of Liberty*.

Circle each geographical name that needs a capital letter.

1. Famous for its golden gate bridge, san francisco lies by the pacific ocean.
2. Famous for its french quarter, new orleans is the last port on the mississippi river.
3. Famous for its liberty bell, philadelphia is in the state of pennsylvania.
4. Famous for tea, rice, and silk, china is the home of the great wall.
5. Famous for its pasta, grapes, and gondolas, italy is the home of the roman coliseum.
6. Famous for safaris and large game preserves, kenya is bordered on the west by lake victoria.

Rewrite two of the sentences above, using correct capitalization.

7. _____ **Answers may vary.** _____

8. _____

98   CD-104310 • © Carson-Dellosa

Name _____

Parts of a Letter

> Letters have five parts: **date, greeting, body, closing,** and **signature**. Capitalize the first word in greetings and closings. Greetings and closings end with commas. The greeting, closing, and signature have their own lines.
>
> Example:
>
> January 2, 2009
>
> Dear Grandpa,
>
> Thank you for taking me fishing. I liked catching all of those fish. They tasted great for dinner. I hope we catch more when we go fishing again.
>
> Love,
>
> Tricia

Fill in the missing parts of these letters. Label each part.

1.

Dear Mike,
You are invited to my house for my birthday party. Please let me know if you can come.

Sincerely,   **Answers may vary (missing: date, signature).**

2.

I went to the library on Monday. I chose five books and listened to a great storyteller. I hope you can meet me there next Monday.

Answers may vary (missing: date, greeting, closing, signature).

CD-104310 • © Carson-Dellosa   99

Answer Key

Name _____ | Letters |

Parts of a Letter

Remember, when writing a letter, capitalize the first word in the greeting.
  Example: Dear neighbor,
Also, capitalize the first word of the closing.
  Examples: Yours truly, Sincerely, Your friend,

1. Circle all of the words below that need capital letters.

(July) 1, 2008

(dear) Aunt Laura,

Thank you so much for the gift card. I am going to use it to buy a game I have been wanting. When you and Uncle Mike come to visit this summer, we can all play my new game.

(your) nephew,

Mickey

2. Fill in the blanks below using correct capitalization.

(date) _____   **Answers may vary.**

(greeting) _____

It was wonderful to see you last week. I'm so glad you could come for a visit. I especially enjoyed our trip to the Science Center. On your next visit, we can go to the museum in town. I hope to see you again soon.

(closing) _____ ,

Dianne

100   CD-104310 • © Carson-Dellosa

Name _____ | Letters |

Friendly Letters and Business Letters

Friendly letters and **business letters** differ in their purposes, but the same capitalization rules apply to both types of letters. In addition to the five parts of a friendly letter—the date, the greeting, the body, the closing, and the signature—a business letter has an inside address.
  Example of a greeting for a friendly letter: Dear Mom and Dad,
  Example of a greeting for a business letter: Dear Toy Palace:
  Example of a closing for a friendly and a business letter: Sincerely,

1. Circle each letter that should be capitalized in the friendly letter.

(a)ugust 1, 2008

(d)ear (b)arbara,

(I) am really enjoying my summer vacation on my uncle's ranch (t)here are horses to ride, and my cousins and (I) go fishing every day (I)'ll see you in two more weeks, and then (I) can show you my pictures.

(y)our friend,

(b)onnie

2. Circle each letter that should be capitalized in the business letter.

4407 (n)inth (s)treet
(h)illside, (m)aine 04024
(m)arch 10, 2008
(s)kateboards and (m)ore
6243 (r)ock (a)ve.
(d)etroit, (m)ichigan 48201
To whom it may concern:

I am returning my skateboard for repair (i)t is still under warranty. (p)lease repair it and return the skateboard to the address above as soon as possible.

(s)incerely,

(s)am (s)mith

CD-104310 • © Carson-Dellosa   101

Name _____ | Letters |

Commas in Letters

When writing a date, use a **comma** (,) to separate the day from the year.
  Example: October 6, 2000
Use an additional comma after the year if it is not the last word in a sentence.
  Example: October 6, 2000, was the date on which Julia was born.
Use a comma to separate the name of a city from the state.
  Example: Toledo, Ohio
Use an additional comma after the name of the state if it is not the last word in a sentence.
  Example: Toledo, Ohio, was Julia's birthplace.
Use a comma after the greeting and after the closing of both a friendly letter and a business letter:
  Examples: Dear Julia, (greeting) Sincerely, (closing)

Write commas in each phrase or sentence where they belong.

1. My family visits Spring Grove Minnesota every year in the summer. **My family visits Spring Grove, Minnesota, every year in the summer.**

2. Dear Grandpa **Dear Grandpa,**

3. Yours truly **Yours truly,**

4. On October 9 2008 Carolyn saw the play. **On October 9, 2008, Carolyn saw the play.**

5. My aunt and uncle live in North Branch New York. **My aunt and uncle live in North Branch, New York.**

6. Dear Jon **Dear Jon,**

7. January 1 2009 **January 1, 2009**

8. Paris Texas is located in the northeast part of the state. **Paris, Texas is located in the northeast part of the state.**

102   CD-104310 • © Carson-Dellosa

Name _____ | Letters |

Writing Letters

Write a friendly letter.

_____
_____   **Answers will vary, but should have**
_____   **all components of a friendly letter.**
_____
_____
_____
_____
_____
_____

Write a business letter.

_____
_____   **Answers will vary, but should have**
_____   **all components of a business letter.**
_____
_____
_____
_____
_____
_____
_____

CD-104310 • © Carson-Dellosa   103

---

128   CD-104310 • © Carson-Dellosa

Congratulations!

receives this award for

Signed

Date

, | adverb | helping verb | imperative

! | adjective | linking verb | exclamatory

? | action verb | proper noun | interrogative

• | noun | pronoun | declarative

Becky	Waldo	Max	Carlos
© CD	© CD	© CD	© CD
New York	Great Britain	Brookstown Mall	Liberty Bell
© CD	© CD	© CD	© CD
I	you	me	we
© CD	© CD	© CD	© CD
she	he	it	they
© CD	© CD	© CD	© CD

us

their

was

might

© CD

© CD

© CD

© CD

them

my

are

have

© CD

© CD

© CD

© CD

her

her

am

has

© CD

© CD

© CD

© CD

him

his

is

were

© CD

© CD

© CD

© CD

seem	where	mice	went
will	an	vacation	vanish
been	the	butterfly	cheerful
could	a	when	migrate

© CD

softer	nice	badly	now
© CD	© CD	© CD	© CD
sweetest	chocolate	bad	at
© CD	© CD	© CD	© CD
heard	blue	good	never
© CD	© CD	© CD	© CD
felt	beautiful	well	sometimes
© CD	© CD	© CD	© CD

I'll

people's

display

lovely

won't

dogs'

hatch

quickly

she'll

Bill's

write

most

can't

children's

bring

more